FRENCH WITHOUT TEARS

Produced at the Criterion Theatre, Piccadilly Circus, London, on November 6th, 1936, with the following cast of characters:

(In the order of their appearance)

KENNETH LAKE	*Trevor Howard.*
BRIAN CURTIS	*Guy Middleton.*
HON. ALAN HOWARD	*Rex Harrison.*
MARIANNE	*Yvonne Andre.*
MONSIEUR MAINGOT	*Percy Walsh.*
LIEUT.-COMMANDER ROGERS	*Roland Culver.*
DIANA LAKE	*Kay Hammond.*
KIT NEILAN	*Robert Flemyng.*
JACQUELINE MAINGOT	*Jessica Tandy.*
LORD HEYBROOK	*Gerald Campion.*

The Play produced by HAROLD FRENCH.

The action passes in the living-room at " Miramar," a villa in a small seaside town in the South of France.

ACT I

A morning in July.

ACT II

SCENE 1.—Two weeks later.   Early afternoon.
SCENE 2.—Six hours later.

ACT III

SCENE 1.—A few hours later.
SCENE 2.—Next morning.

FRENCH WITHOUT TEARS

ACT I

SCENE.—*The living-room at " Miramar," a villa in a small seaside town in the South of France.*

TIME.—*July 1st, about 9 a.m.*

The room is adequately furnished. There is a large oak table in the c. surrounded by five small chairs. At the front of the table is a long upholstered bench to seat three. There are two upholstered armchairs, one down L. and one down R. At the back in the alcove is a large bookcase containing French dictionaries, phrase-books, etc., and other " works." In front of the bookcase is a settee in keeping with the other furniture. The wallpaper is sea-green spaced with a medallion of a deeper green. The room appears to have been lived in, though bright and well kept. There are two electric candle-brackets of the Louis XV period, with pink shades, on each side of the bookcase alcove.

The table is laid for breakfast, with an enormous coffee-pot in the middle and a quantity of rolls.

As the CURTAIN *rises* KENNETH *is* R.C. *making signals. He is about twenty; good-looking in a vacuous way. He walks up towards the window* R.*, then back, and then down to seat 6, which is below the table* C. *He sits. A phrase-book and dictionary lie open before him.*

There is the sound of someone heavily descending the stairs. The door up L. *opens and* BRIAN *comes in. He is older than* KENNETH, *about twenty-three or twenty-four, large, thick-set and red-faced. He wears an incredibly dirty pair of grey flannel trousers, a battered brown tweed coat, and a white sweater.*

BRIAN. Morning, Babe.

(KENNETH *doesn't look up.* BRIAN *comes down to the table, chair 2, picks up a letter and opens it.*)

KENNETH (*looking musingly ahead*). She has ideas above her station.

BRIAN. What's that ?

KENNETH. How would you say that in French ?

7

BRIAN. What?

KENNETH. She has ideas above her station.

BRIAN. She has ideas above her station. She has ideas——
(*He stuffs his letter in his pocket and goes to the door down* L., *calling.*)
Marianne.

VOICE (*from the kitchen*). Oui, monsieur?

BRIAN (*with an appalling accent*). Deux œufs, s'il vous plaît.

VOICE (*off*). Bien, monsieur.

BRIAN. Avec un petit peu de jambon.

VOICE (*off*). Oui, monsieur. Des œufs brouillés, n'est-ce pas?

BRIAN. Brouillés? Ah, oui, brouillés. (*He closes the door,
returns to chair* 2 *and puts sugar in his cup.*) I'm getting pretty
hot at this stuff, don't you think? You know, nowadays it's quite
an effort for me to go back to English.

KENNETH. If you're so hot you'd better tell me how to say
she has ideas above her station.

BRIAN (*taking his cup to* C. *of the table*). Oh, yes, I forgot. It's
fairly easy, old boy. Elle a des idées au-dessus de sa gare.

KENNETH. You can't do it like that. You can't say au-dessus
de sa gare. It isn't that sort of station.

BRIAN. Well, don't *ask* me.

KENNETH. I thought you were so hot at French.

BRIAN (*pouring out coffee*). Well, as a matter of fact, that wasn't
strictly the truth. Now if a Frenchman asked me where the pen
of his aunt was, the chances are I could give him a pretty snappy
come-back, and tell him it was in the pocket of the gardener.

KENNETH. Yes, but that doesn't help me much.

BRIAN. Sorry, old boy.

KENNETH. I suppose I'd better just do it literally. Maingot'll
throw a fit.

BRIAN. That doesn't bother you, does it? (*He picks up his
cup and puts it at his place, chair* 2.)

KENNETH. You're not going into the diplomatic. He doesn't
really get worked up about you.

BRIAN (*going to the table up* R. *and taking a banana*). Well, I
don't know about that. The whole of his beard came off yesterday
when I was having my lesson. (*He returns to chair* 2 *and starts to
eat the banana.*)

KENNETH. No, but he doesn't really mind. It's absolute
physical agony to him when I do something wrong. He knows
as well as I do that I haven't got one chance in a thousand of
getting in.

BRIAN (*cheerfully*). Don't say that, old boy, you're breaking my
heart.

KENNETH (*gloomily*). Yes, but it's true. (*He returns to the study
of his book.*)

BRIAN (*sitting*). As a matter of fact, Alan told me you had a
pretty good chance.

KENNETH (*looking up, pleased*). Did he really ?

(BRIAN *nods.*)

BRIAN. He ought to know, oughtn't he ? Isn't he Maingot's red-hot tip for the diplomatic stakes ?

KENNETH. If he was keener about getting in he'd walk it. He will, anyway, I should think.

BRIAN. I think I'll make a book on the result this year. I'll lay evens on Alan—a class colt with a nice free action. Will win if he can get the distance.

KENNETH. What about me ?

BRIAN. I'll lay you threes about yourself.

KENNETH. Threes ? More like twenties.

BRIAN. Oh, I don't know. Nice-looking colt—good stayer. Bit of a dog from the starting-gate, perhaps. Say seven to two, then.

(ALAN *enters through the door up* L. *He is about twenty-three, dark and saturnine. He wears carefully creased grey flannel trousers and a German " sport jacket."*)

Morning, Alan. We were just talking about you.

ALAN. Good morning, Brian. Good morning, Babe. (*He goes to his place at the head of the table, chair* 1, *and deposits "The Times."*) Not one blood-stained letter. (*He speaks slowly and rather pedantically.*) What were you saying about me ? (*He takes his cup round to* L. *end of the table, pours himself out milk and coffee and then moves back to chair* 1.)

BRIAN. I'm making a book on the diplomatic stakes. I'm laying evens about you.

ALAN. That's not very generous.

BRIAN. Hell, you're the favourite.

ALAN. What about the startling rumours that the favourite may be scratched ?

KENNETH (*looking up quickly*). Why, have they accepted your novel ?

ALAN. Do I look as if they'd accepted my novel ?

BRIAN. I don't know how you do look when they accept your novels.

ALAN (*patting* BRIAN *on the shoulder and sitting chair* 1). I hope, my dear Brian, that one day you'll have a chance of finding out.

KENNETH. Well, what's this talk about your scratching ?

ALAN. Perhaps just to give you a better chance, ducky.

BRIAN. You're not serious about it though, old boy ?

ALAN. Probably not.

KENNETH. But you must be mad, Alan. I mean even if you do want to write you could still do it in the diplomatic. Honestly, it seems quite crazy——

ALAN.   You're giving a tolerably good imitation of my father. (*To* BRIAN.)   Pass the sugar.

BRIAN (*passing the cream*).   What does His Excellency have to say about the idea, by the way ?

ALAN.   Sugar, half-wit.

(BRIAN *passes the sugar.*)

His Excellency says that he doesn't mind me choosing my own career a bit, provided always it's the one he's chosen for me.

BRIAN.   Broad-minded, eh ?

ALAN.   That's right.   Always sees two sides to every question —his own, which is the right one, and anyone else's, which is the wrong one.

KENNETH.   But seriously, Alan, you can't really be thinking——

ALAN.   Oh, stop it, child, for God's sake.   I didn't say I was going to scratch.

KENNETH.   You said you were thinking of it.

ALAN.   Well, you know that I'm always thinking of it.   I very rarely think of anything else.   But I won't do it, so don't worry your dear little head about it.

(KENNETH *sulkily returns to his work.*   MARIANNE, *the maid, enters down* L. *with a plate of scrambled eggs and places them in front of* BRIAN.)

BRIAN.   Ah, mes œufs, as I live.

MARIANNE (*between chairs* 2 *and* 3—*to* BRIAN).   Monsieur le Commandant, va-t-il aussi prendre des œufs avec son petit déjeuner, monsieur ?

BRIAN.   Oh, well—er—she's talking to you, old boy.

ALAN.   Je ne sais rien des habitudes de Monsieur le Commandant, Marianne.

MARIANNE.   Bien, monsieur.   (*She turns to go, then stops.*) Alors voulez-vous lui demander s'il les veut, monsieur, lorsqu'il descend ?

ALAN.   Bien.

MARIANNE.   Bien, monsieur.

(*She exits down* L.)

BRIAN.   What did she want ?

ALAN.   She wanted to know if the Commander took eggs with his breakfast.

BRIAN.   I meant to ask you.   Did you see him when he arrived last night ?

ALAN.   Yes, I went to the station with Maingot to meet him.

BRIAN.   What's he like ?

ALAN.   Very naval commander.

BRIAN.   Yes, old boy, but what's that ?

ALAN.   You know.   Carries with him the salty tang of the sea wherever he goes.

BRIAN. Pity he's carried it here. Paucot-sur-Mer could do without any more salty tang than it's got already. Has he a rolling gait ?

ALAN. He was sober when he arrived.

BRIAN. No, old boy, drunk or sober, all sailors have a rolling gait.

(MONSIEUR MAINGOT *comes in hurriedly through the door* up L., *carrying a cup of coffee. He is about sixty, with a ferocious face and a dark beard. All three rise.*)

MAINGOT (*shaking hands all round*). Bonjour ! Bonjour ! Bonjour ! (*He sits down at the head of the table, chair 5, and puts his cup down.*) Mon Dieu, que je suis en retard ce matin ! (*He opens a letter and reads.*)

(*The others have sat down again.*)

BRIAN (*speaking in a whisper to* ALAN). What's he like, though, really ?

ALAN (*also in a whisper*). Pretty hellish, I thought.

BRIAN. Po-faced, I suppose ?

MAINGOT (*roaring into his letter*). Français ! Voulez-vous parler français, messieurs, s'il vous plaît.

(*There is a pause.*)

(*Looking up from his letter.*) Qu'est-ce que ça veut dire, po-faced ?

ALAN. Nous disions que Monsieur le Commandant avait une figure de vase de nuit, monsieur.

MAINGOT. Ah, ce n'est pas vrai.

ALAN. Nous exaggérons un peu.

MAINGOT. Je crois bien.

(MAINGOT *grunts and returns to his letter.*)

(KENNETH *surreptitiously pushes his notebook towards* ALAN, *pointing at a certain sentence.* ALAN *reads it and shakes his head violently.* KENNETH *looks pleadingly at him.* ALAN *considers, and is about to speak when* MAINGOT *looks up.*)

Dites-moi, est-ce-que vous connaissez un Lord Heybrook ?

ALAN. Non, monsieur.

MAINGOT (*looking at the letter*). Il voudrait venir le quinze juillet.

ALAN (*to* BRIAN). Do you know him ?

BRIAN. Lord Heybrook ? No, old boy. (*Confidentially.*) As a matter of fact, I knew a peer once, but he died. What about Lord Heybrook, anyway ?

ALAN. He's coming here on the fifteenth.

MAINGOT (*roaring*). Français, messieurs—français !

(*There is a pause.* MAINGOT *takes up " Le Matin " and begins to read.* KENNETH *again pushes his notebook towards* ALAN *and* ALAN *again is about to speak.*)

(*Reading his paper.*)   Ah!   Ce Hitler!   (*Throwing the paper on the floor.*)   Quel phénomène!

(ALAN *closes his mouth and* KENNETH *pulls his notebook back quickly.*)

(*To* BRIAN.)   Ah, Monsieur Curtis, vous étiez saôul au casino hier soir, n'est-ce pas?
  BRIAN (*puzzled*).   Saôul?
  ALAN.   Drunk.
  BRIAN.   Oh, non, monsieur.   Pas ça.   Un peu huilé, peut-être.

(COMMANDER ROGERS *comes in up* L.   *He is about thirty-five, dark, small, very neat, rather solemn.   All get up.*)

  MAINGOT.   Ah!   Bonjour, Monsieur le Commandant, et comment allez vous?   J'espère que vous avez bien dormi?   Ah, pardon!   (*He introduces the others.*)   Monsieur Curtis—Monsieur le Commandant Rogers.   Monsieur Lake—Monsieur le Commandant Rogers—Monsieur Howard vous connaissez déjà.

(BRIAN *and* KENNETH *shake hands.*   ALAN *nods and smiles.*)

  ALAN.   Bonjour.
  ROGERS.   Yes, we met last night.   (*Indicating chair* 3.)   Shall I sit here?

(KENNETH *goes on to the veranda.*   MAINGOT *picks up his paper from the floor.*)

  ALAN.   That's Kit Neilan's place, as a matter of fact.   I think this is your place.   (*He shows a place next to* MAINGOT.)
  MAINGOT.   Ah!   Pardon, Monsieur le Commandant.   Voilà votre place.   (*He shows him chair* 4.)   Asseyez-vous donc et soyez à votre aise.   (*He sits.*)

(BRIAN *and* ALAN *reseat themselves.*)

  ROGERS.   Thanks.   (*He sits.*)
  ALAN.   I've been told to ask you if you like eggs with your breakfast.
  MAINGOT.   Oui, monsieur, mais voulez-vous parler français, s'il vous plaît.
  ROGERS (*smiling apologetically*).   I'm afraid I don't speak your lingo at all, you know.
  MAINGOT.   Lingo?   Ah oui, langue.   C'est ça, mais il faut essayer.   You—must—try.
  ROGERS (*turning to* MAINGOT, *then to* ALAN).   Oui—Non.
  ALAN.   What?
  MAINGOT.   Pardon!
  ROGERS.   Oui, je ne—want any eggs.
  ALAN.   Right, I'll tell Marianne.   (*He gets up and goes into the kitchen down* L.)

MAINGOT (*to* ROGERS).   Il faut dire : Je ne veux pas d'œufs pour mon petit déjeuner.

(ROGERS *smiles vaguely.*   MAINGOT *laughs.*)

Ça viendra, ça viendra.

(ALAN *returns and sits in chair* 1.)

BRIAN.   I say, sir.   Did you have a good crossing ?

ROGERS.   Pretty bad, as a matter of fact.   Still, that didn't worry me.

BRIAN.   You're a good sailor ?

(ALAN *laughs.*)

Oh, of course, you would be.   I mean you are, aren't you ?   Damn silly, old boy!

MAINGOT.   Eh bien.   Par qui vais-je commencer ?

KENNETH (*from the veranda*).   Moi, monsieur.

MAINGOT.   *Par* moi.   (*Rising.*)   Alors, allons dans le jardin. (*He crosses to the window* R., *bows and says :*)   Messieurs !

(*They all rise.*   ALAN *and* ROGERS *sit again after* MAINGOT *has gone. He is followed by* KENNETH.   BRIAN *stays up by the window* R.)

ALAN.   Poor Babe.   He's going to be slaughtered.

ROGERS (*helping himself to breakfast*).   Really ?   Why ?

ALAN (*shaking his head sadly*).   Elle a des idées au-dessus de sa gare.

ROGERS.   What does that mean ?

ALAN.   It doesn't mean she has ideas above her station.

ROGERS.   The Professor is pretty strict, I suppose.

ALAN.   Where work is concerned he's a sadist.

ROGERS.   I'm glad to hear it.   I want to learn as much French as I can, and I'm starting from scratch, you know.

BRIAN.   Are you learning it for any special reason, sir ?

ROGERS.   Yes.   Interpretership exam. in seven months' time.

ALAN.   If you stay here for seven months, you'll either be dead or a Frenchman.

ROGERS.   How long have you been here ?

ALAN.   On and off for a year, but then I have a way of preserving my nationality.   I wear a special charm.   (*He indicates his German coat.*)

ROGERS.   Are you very pro-German, then ?

BRIAN (*speaking from the steps up* R.).   He only wears that coat to annoy Maingot.

ROGERS.   Oh, I see.   What do you wear in Germany ?

ALAN.   A beret usually.   Sabots are too uncomfortable.

(ROGERS *laughs politely.   There is a pause, broken suddenly by a roar coming from the garden.*)

MAINGOT (*off*). Ah, ça c'est formidable ! Qu'est-ce que vous me fichez là donc ? " Elle a des idées au-dessus de sa gare." Idiot ! Idiot ! Idiot !

(*ALAN rises and goes up to join* BRIAN *at the window. The noise subsides.* ALAN *shakes his head.*)

ALAN (*returning to chair 1 and sitting*). Poor Babe. But he had it coming to him.

BRIAN (*coming down to behind chair 2*). The Babe was having the horrors this morning before you came down. He said he hadn't one chance in a thousand of getting in.

ALAN. He hasn't.

ROGERS. Of getting in what ?

ALAN. The diplomatic.

ROGERS. Oh, I suppose you're all budding diplomats ?

BRIAN. All except me. I'm learning French for—er—commercial reasons.

ALAN. He's learnt a lot already. He can say " How much ? " in French, and you know how valuable that phrase is in the world of—er—commerce.

BRIAN (*laughing heartily*). Yes, old boy, and that's not all. I can say " Five francs ? Do you think I'm made of money ? "

ALAN (*laughing too*). " Cinq francs ? Crois-tu que je sois construit d'argent ? "

(*They both suddenly become aware that* ROGERS *isn't laughing. They stop and there is rather an awkward pause.* BRIAN *goes to the armchair down* R. *and sits.*)

BRIAN (*signalling*). Pie-faced.

ROGERS (*with a wooden face*). Who else is staying here at the moment ?

ALAN. There's only Kit Neilan, I think, that you haven't met.

ROGERS. Oh ! Is he going into the diplomatic too ?

ALAN. Yes. (*To* BRIAN.) By the way, Brian, what odds did you lay against Kit in your book ?

BRIAN. I didn't, but I should think five to two against would about meet the case.

ALAN. I don't know. The odds must have lengthened considerably these last few weeks.

BRIAN. Why ? Oh, you mean Diana. I say old boy, I hadn't thought of that. You don't think there's a chance of a well-fancied colt being withdrawn before the big contest ?

ALAN. No. She won't marry him. That is, not until she's exhausted other possibilities. (*He rises and fetches a book from the bookcase up* C.)

ROGERS. Er—who is this girl ?

BRIAN. Diana ? She's Babe's—Kenneth Lake's sister. She's staying here.

ROGERS. Oh! is she learning French too ?

BRIAN. No. She just stops us from learning it. No, she's staying here because her people live in India and she's got nowhere else to go.

ROGERS. Pretty dull for her here, I should think.

ALAN (*returning to his seat*). That girl wouldn't find it dull on a desert island.

BRIAN. Unless it *was* deserted.

ALAN. True. But one feels somehow it wouldn't be deserted long if she were on it.

ROGERS. What do you mean by that ?

ALAN. I've no idea. She's a nice girl. You'll love her.

(BRIAN *hides a smile.*)

At least, it won't be her fault if you don't.

ROGERS (*politely*). I don't quite follow you, I'm afraid.

ALAN. I'm sorry, sir. I was forgetting you're of an age to take care of yourself.

ROGERS (*testily*). There's no need to call me sir, you know.

(ALAN *raises his eyebrows.*)

What you're implying is that this girl is—er—rather fast.

ALAN. I'm not implying it. I'm saying it. That girl is the fastest worker you're ever likely to see.

ROGERS. Oh! (*He goes back to his food.*)

BRIAN (*conciliatorily*). What he means is that she's just naturally full of joie de vivre and all that. She's all right really. She just likes company.

ALAN (*under his breath*). A battalion, you mean.

ROGERS. You sound embittered.

ALAN. Embittered ? Oh, no. Oh, dear me, no. (*He breaks a roll open rather violently.*) Both Brian and I, for reasons that I won't go into now, are immune. Only I thought it just as well to let you know before you met her that Diana Lake, though a dear girl in many ways, is a little unreliable in her emotional life.

ROGERS. You mean she isn't in love with this chap Kit What's-his-name who wants to marry her.

ALAN. The only reason I have for supposing she isn't is that she says that she is. But that's good enough for me.

(BRIAN *jumps up from the armchair down* R., *crosses to the bookcase* C. *and takes a book.*)

BRIAN. Well, Maingot's simple French Phrases are calling me.

ROGERS (*evidently glad to change the subject*). Maingot's phrase-book. He's given me that to do too.

BRIAN. Good. Then very soon now you will be able to walk

into a chemist's and say in faultless French, " Please, sir, I wish a toothpaste with a slightly stronger scent."

Rogers. Oh, really ?

Alan. Then think how nice it'll be if you're in a railway carriage and you're able to inform a fellow traveller that the guard has just waved a red flag to signify that the locomotive has run off the line.

Rogers. Sounds a bit out of date, I must say.

Brian. Maingot's grandfather wrote it, I believe.

(*The telephone rings.* Brian *turns round.*)

Do you know, I have a nasty feeling that's Chi-Chi.

Rogers. Who's Chi-Chi ?

Brian. That's not her real name.

(Maingot's *voice is heard from the garden.*)

Maingot (*off*). Monsieur Howard.

Alan (*calling*). Oui, monsieur ?

Maingot (*off*). Voulez-vous repondre au telephone, s'il vous plaît ?

Alan. Bien, monsieur. (*He rises.*)

Maingot. Merci.

(Alan *crosses below the table to the 'phone, and takes off the receiver.*)

Alan. Hullo . . . Bien. Attendez. (*He holds out the receiver to* Brian.)

Brian. Me ? Hell !

(Brian *comes and takes the receiver, giving a piece of buttered bread and a book to* Alan. Alan *returns to chair* 1.)

Hullo . . . Ah, hullo, Chi-Chi. Comment ça va ? Comment-allez-vous ? Quoi ? Quoi ? Wait a moment, Chi-Chi. (*He lowers the receiver.*) Take it for me, old boy. I can't hear a word the girl's saying.

(Alan *comes and takes it.* Brian *goes to above chair* 3.)

Alan. Hullo . . . Oui, il ne comprend pas . . . Bien. Je le lui demanderai. (*To* Brian.) Can you see her to-night at the Casino ? She wants you to meet her sister.

Brian. Ask her if it's the same one I met on Tuesday.

Alan (*into the 'phone*). Il voudrait savoir s'il a déjà rencontré votre sœur. . . . Bon. (*To* Brian.) She says it's a different one.

Brian. Tell her it's O.K. I'll be there.

Alan (*into the 'phone*). Il dit qu'il sera enchanté. . . . Oui. Au revoir. (*He hangs up the receiver and comes to* ʟ. *of chair* 5.)

Brian. I told that damn woman not to ring up here.

(Maingot *enters through the window and comes to up* ʀ.ᴏ.)

MAINGOT.   Alors ; qui est ce qui vient de telephoner ?

BRIAN (*apologetically*).   C'était quelqu'un pour moi, monsieur.

MAINGOT.   Pour vous ?

BRIAN.   Oui, une fille que je connais dans la ville.

MAINGOT.   Une fille ! (*He bursts into a stentorian roar of laughter and goes back into the garden.*)   Une fille qu'il connaît ! Ho ! Ho !

BRIAN.   Now what's bitten him ?

ALAN.   A fille doesn't mean a girl, Brian.

BRIAN.   It says so in my dictionary.   What does it mean, then ?

ALAN.   A tart.

BRIAN.   Oh ! (*He considers a second.*)   Well, I hate to have to say it, old boy, but having a strict regard for the truth, that's a fairly neat little description of Chi-Chi.   See you two at lunch-time.

(*He goes out through the doors up L.*)

ALAN.   There in a nutshell you have the reason for Brian's immunity to the charms of Diana Lake.

ROGERS (*icily*).   Really ?

ALAN (*easily*).   Yes.   (*He crosses to the table up R., takes a cigarette and lights it.*)   This place is going to be rather a change for you after your boat, isn't it ?

ROGERS (*stung*).   You mean my ship, don't you ?

ALAN.   Oh, is there a difference ?

ROGERS.   There is.

ALAN.   Of course.   (*Coming to chair 2.*)   It's a grave social error to say boat for ship, isn't it ?   Like mentioning a lady's name before the royal toast or talking about Harrow College.   (*He goes and sits in chair 1.*)

ROGERS.   Yes, that would be very wrong.

(DIANA LAKE *comes in from the garden.   She is in a bathing-wrap which she wears open, disclosing a bathing-dress underneath.   She is about twenty, very lovely.*)

DIANA.   Good morning. (*She stops at the sight of* ROGERS *and decorously pulls her wrap more closely about her.*)

(ROGERS *and* ALAN *get up.*)

ALAN.   Good morning, Diana.   I don't think you've met Commander Rogers.

DIANA (*coming to above chair* 3).   How-do-you-do ?

ROGERS.   How-do-you-do ?

(*They shake hands.*)

DIANA (*to* ROGERS).   I didn't know you'd—you must have arrived last night, I suppose.

ALAN (*sitting*).   Don't you remember ?   You asked me what train he was coming by.

DIANA.   Do sit down, Commander Rogers.

(*He sits.*)

How are you this morning, Alan ?

ALAN. Oh, very well, thank you. I'll bet you didn't go in the water.

DIANA. Yes, I did.

ALAN. Right in ?

DIANA. Yes, right in. Ask Kit.

ALAN (*really surprised*). Kit ! You don't mean to say that you got Kit to go bathing with you ?

DIANA. Yes, I did. He's fetching my towel. I left it behind.

ALAN. God ! You women.

DIANA. What ?

ALAN. Without the slightest qualm and just to gratify a passing whim, you force a high-souled young man to shatter one of his most sacred principles.

ROGERS. What principle is that, if I might ask ?

DIANA (*emphatically, standing by chair 2*). Never, under any circumstances, to do anything hearty. (*She goes up* C., *leaves her sunglasses on the bookshelf and returns to chair 2.*)

ROGERS (*challengingly*). Personally, I rather like an early morning dip. (*He lights a cigarette.*)

(ALAN *exchanges glances with* DIANA.)

ALAN (*as if the words burnt his mouth*). An—early—morning—dip ?

ROGERS. Certainly. That's hearty, I suppose.

ALAN. Well——

DIANA. I quite agree with you, Commander Rogers. I don't think there's anything nicer than a swim before breakfast. Ashtray ? (*She hands one to* ROGERS *from the table up* R.)

ALAN. You'd like anything that gave you a chance to come down to breakfast in a bathing-dress.

DIANA. Does it shock you, Alan ?

ALAN. Unutterably.

DIANA. I'll go and dress, then. (*She moves towards the door up* L.)

ALAN. No. There's no point in that. You've made one successful entrance. Don't spoil it by making another.

ROGERS. I don't think I quite understand you.

ALAN. Diana does, don't you, angel ?

(DIANA *takes an apple from the table up* R.)

DIANA (*sweetly*). Has another publisher refused your novel, Alan ? (*She crosses to the armchair down* R. *and sits.*)

(ALAN, *momentarily disconcerted, can find nothing to say. There is a pause.*

Enter KIT *through the French windows. He is about twenty-two, fair and good looking. He wears a dressing-gown over his bathing-dress, and carries two towels over his arm.*)

KIT (*sullenly*). Morning. (*He comes to above chair* **3.**)
ALAN (*in gentle reproof*). Well, well, well.
KIT (*shamefacedly*). Well, why not ?

(ALAN *shakes his head sadly.*)

ALAN. I don't think you've met Commander Rogers.
KIT (*shaking hands*). How-do-you-do ? I heard you were coming. (*He sits in chair* **3.**)
ALAN. Did Diana go in the water ?
KIT. No.
DIANA. Kit, you dirty liar.
KIT. I've done enough for you already this morning. I'm not going to perjure myself as well. I had hoped you wouldn't be here, Alan, to witness my shame.
ALAN. You of all people an early morning dipper.
KIT (*shuddering*). Don't put it like that. You make it sound worse than it is. Say a nine-o'clock bather. (*He picks up the coffee-pot.*) Oh, hell, this coffee's cold. (*Calling.*) Marianne !
ALAN. Mere toying with words can't hide the truth. Do you know, I think that girl could make you go for a bicycle tour in the Pyrenees if she set her mind to it.
KIT. She could, you know, Alan, that's the awful thing.

(*There is a slight pause.*)

ROGERS. I once went for a bicycle tour in the Pyrenees.
ALAN. Really ?

(JACQUELINE *comes out of the kitchen. She is about twenty-five or twenty-six, not unattractive, but nothing in looks to compare with* DIANA. *She wears an apron, and has a handkerchief tied over her hair.*)

JACQUELINE. Marianne's upstairs. Do you want anything ? (*She speaks with only the barest trace of accent.*)
KIT. Hello, Jack.
ALAN. Good morning, darling.
JACQUELINE (*going to* ROGERS). How-do-you-do, Commander Rogers. I'm so glad you could come to us.
ROGERS (*rising and shaking hands*). Er—how-do-you-do ?
JACQUELINE. I hope you've found everything you want.
ROGERS. Yes, thank you.
JACQUELINE (*coming round below the table and starting to clear some of the plates*). Did Marianne ask you if you wanted eggs for breakfast ?
ROGERS. I don't want any, thanks.
JACQUELINE. I see. Well, don't worry about asking for anything you need. By the way, do you drink beer at meals or do you prefer wine ? (*She is now between chairs* 1 *and* 2.)
ROGERS (*sitting*). Beer, please. Nothing like a can of beer.

ALAN. No, I suppose there isn't.

JACQUELINE (*above chair* 2, *to* KIT). What were you shouting about, by the way ?

KIT. Jack, darling, the coffee's cold.

JACQUELINE. Of course it's cold. You're half an hour late for breakfast.

KIT. Yes, but——

JACQUELINE. You can't have any more, because Marianne's doing the rooms.

KIT (*rising*). I thought perhaps, Jack, darling, knowing how much you love me, you might be an angel and do something about it.

JACQUELINE. Certainly not.

(KIT *sits.*)

It's against all the rules of the house. Besides, you'd better go and get dressed. I'm giving you a lesson in five minutes.

KIT. In the near future, when I am Minister of Foreign Affairs, this incident will play a large part in my decision to declare war on France.

JACQUELINE (*grabbing the coffee-pot*). Ooh! This is the last time I'm going to do this for you.

(JACQUELINE *exits into the kitchen.*)

KIT (*to* DIANA). You see what a superb diplomat I should make.

ALAN. Rather the Palmerston tradition, wasn't it ?

ROGERS. Was that Maingot's daughter ?

KIT. Yes. Her name's Jacqueline.

ROGERS. Jacqueline ? (*Brightly.*) I see. That's why you call her Jack.

KIT (*looking at him distastefully*). Yes, that's why we call her Jack.

ROGERS. She speaks English very well.

KIT. She's been in England half her life. I believe she's going to be an English school-marm. You'll like her. She's amusing. (*He continues to dry himself.*) Hell! I still feel wet.

(DIANA *rises, goes to chair* 2 *and sits.*)

DIANA. You've got such lovely hair, darling. That's why it takes so long to dry.

KIT (*to* ALAN). You know, Alan, this is a nice girl.

ALAN (*tilting his chair back and gazing at* DIANA). Yes, she's nice. She's good, too.

(DIANA *is drying* KIT'S *hair, burying his head in the towel.* ROGERS *gets up.*)

ROGERS. Well, I must go upstairs. I want to get my room shipshape.

ALAN. And above board ?

ROGERS (*turning savagely on* ALAN). Yes, and above board. **Any** objection ?

ALAN (*airily*). No, no objection at all. Make it as above board as you like.

ROGERS (*bowing stiffly*). Thank you. I'm most grateful.

(ROGERS *exits up* L.)

ALAN (*pensively*). Do you know, I don't think he likes me.

KIT (*uncovering his head*). Who does ? I'm the only one who can stand you and then only in small doses.

DIANA (*covering* KIT's *head again*). Kenneth adores you, anyway. He's quite silly the way he tries to imitate you.

ALAN. Your brother shows remarkable acumen sometimes.

DIANA. And then, of course, I adore you too. You know that.

(KIT *uncovers his head and takes h er hands.*)

KIT. Hey ! I'm not going to have you adoring anybody except me. Do you understand ? (*He kisses her.*)

DIANA. Darling, you're not jealous of Alan, are you ?

KIT. I'm jealous of anyone you even look at.

DIANA. All right, then in future I won't look at anyone except you.

KIT. That's a promise.

DIANA. That's a promise.

(ALAN, *still leaning back in his chair, whistles a tune softly.*)

(*Feeling* KIT's *hands.*) Darling, you are cold.

KIT. Yes, I know. (*He rises, pushes his chair in, then takes* DIANA *by her hands and pulls her up.*) I think I'll go and dress and not wait for the coffee. You've probably given me pneumonia. But I don't mind. You could tear me up in little pieces and trample on them, and I'd still love you.

DIANA. Sweet little thing. Take these things upstairs, darling, will you ? (*She gives him the towels.*)

(KIT *exits up* L. DIANA *smiles at* ALAN.)

ALAN. That's no reason why you should, you know. (*He rises to above chair 2.*)

DIANA (*above chair 3*). Should what ?

ALAN. Tear him up in little pieces and trample on them.

(DIANA *crosses below* ALAN, *flicking his coat-lapel, then to the window up* R.)

So you're not going to look at anyone except Kit ?

(DIANA *doesn't answer.* ALAN *walks over to the window. He puts his arm round her waist and his cheek against hers.*)

(*After a pause.*) This doesn't mean I'm falling for you.

DIANA (*gently*). Doesn't it, Alan?

ALAN. No, it doesn't. (*He comes to the table, puts his cigarette in the ashtray and then moves down to the armchair* R.)

DIANA. I am disappointed.

ALAN. What do you think of the Commander?

DIANA. I think he's quite nice.

ALAN (*gently*). Yes, I want to tell you, it's no good starting anything with him. (*He sits in the armchair.*)

DIANA. Don't be silly, Alan.

ALAN. It really isn't any good, darling, because you see I've warned him against you.

DIANA. You warned him? (*Coming to* ALAN.) What did you say?

ALAN. I told him what you are.

DIANA (*quietly*). What's that?

ALAN. Don't you know?

DIANA (*sitting* L. *of* ALAN, *on the floor*). Alan, much as I like you, there *are* times when I could cheerfully strangle you.

ALAN. Is this one of them, darling?

DIANA. Yes, ducky, it is.

ALAN. Good, that's just what I hoped.

DIANA. This is rather a new rôle for you, isn't it, playing wet nurse to the Navy?

ALAN. You don't think it suits me?

DIANA. No, darling, I'm afraid I don't. What are you doing it for?

ALAN. It's not because I'm fond of the Commander. As a matter of fact, it would rather amuse me to see you play Hell with him. But I do like Kit, that's why. So no hanky-panky with the Navy or——

DIANA. Or what?

ALAN. Or I shall have to be rather beastly to you, darling, and you know how you wouldn't like that.

DIANA. You don't understand me at all, Alan.

ALAN. I understand every little bit of you, Diana, through and through. That's why we get along so well together.

DIANA (*tearfully*). I ought to hate you.

ALAN (*patting her arm*). Well, go on trying, darling, and you may succeed. I've got to go and finish some stuff for Maingot. See you at lunch-time.

(*He rises and crosses to the door up* L. DIANA *rises to chair* 1.)

DIANA. Alan.

ALAN (*turning at the door*). Yes?

DIANA. What do you mean by hanky-panky?

ALAN. *I* should tell *you*.

(ALAN *exits up* L. DIANA *kicks petulantly at the chair.* JACQUELINE *enters from the kitchen with the coffee-pot. She comes to above chair* 5 *and puts it at* L. *end of the table.*)

DIANA. Oh, thank you so much.

JACQUELINE. Where's Kit ?

DIANA. He's gone up to dress. He felt cold.

JACQUELINE. Isn't that like him ! Well, you can tell him that I'm not going to make him any more coffee, however loud he screams.

DIANA. Yes, I'll tell him, and I think you're quite right.

(ROGERS *enters through the door up* L.)

ROGERS (*nervously*). Oh, hullo.

(JACQUELINE *exits into the kitchen.*)

DIANA (*brightly*). Hullo, Commander Rogers.

(ROGERS *goes over to the bookcase at the back.*)

Looking for something ? (*She moves up to* R. *of him.*)

ROGERS. Yes, Maingot's phrase-book, as a matter of fact. (*He bends down and pulls a book out.*) Here it is, I think. (*He looks at the title.*) No, it isn't.

DIANA. Let me help you. I think I know where it is.

ROGERS. Oh, that's very good of you.

(DIANA *bends down at the bookcase and pulls a book out.*)

DIANA. Here. (*She hands it to him.*)

ROGERS. Oh, thanks most awfully.

DIANA (*going back to the table*). Well, what are your first impressions of Monsieur Maingot's establishment ?

ROGERS. Oh, I—er—think it ought to be very cheery here. (*He half turns to go.*)

DIANA. I'm sure you'll love it.

ROGERS. Yes, I'm sure I will. (*He attempts to go.*)

DIANA. The boys are so nice, don't you think ?

ROGERS. Er—yes, I think they are—some of them. (*He makes a tentative move towards the door again.*)

DIANA (*quickly*). I suppose you find Alan a bit startling, don't you ?

ROGERS. Alan ?

DIANA. The one with the German coat.

ROGERS. Oh, yes. Yes, he is a bit startling. Well, I ought to be getting along. (*He makes another move.*)

DIANA. Why ? You've got your room pretty well shipshape by now, haven't you ?

ROGERS. Oh, thanks, yes, I have.

DIANA. Well, don't go for a bit. (*She comes to chair 4 and sits.*) Stay and talk to me while I have my coffee. Have you got a cigarette ?

ROGERS (*coming to her*). Yes, I have. (*He puts his book down on the table and offers her one.*)

DIANA (*taking one*). Thanks. I was saying about Alan——

ROGERS.   Match ?

DIANA.   Thanks.   (*After he has lighted her cigarette.*)   What was I saying ?

ROGERS.   About Alan.

DIANA.   Oh, yes, about Alan—(*she takes the match from* ROGERS *and puts it in the ashtray*)—he's really very nice, but you mustn't take everything he says seriously.

ROGERS.   Oh ! Oh, I see.   No, I won't.

DIANA.   He's just the tiniest bit—you know (*she taps her forehead significantly*) unbalanced.

ROGERS (*standing* L. *of chair* 5).   Oh, really ?

DIANA.   I thought it as well to warn you.

ROGERS.   Yes.   Thank you very much.

DIANA.   Otherwise it might lead to trouble.

ROGERS.   Yes, it might.

(*There is a pause.*)

DIANA.   Poor Alan.   I'm afraid he's got it very badly.

ROGERS.   Er—got what ?

DIANA.   Well—— (*She leans back and blows a puff of smoke into the air.*)   Of course I oughtn't to say it——

(*She throws him a quick glance to see if he has caught her meaning. Evidently he hasn't.*)

ROGERS.   Oh !

DIANA.   I'm awfully sorry for him of course.

ROGERS (*puzzled, but polite*).   Of course.

DIANA.   It's so funny, because from the way he behaves to me and the things he says about me, you'd think he hated me, wouldn't you ?

ROGERS.   Yes, you would.   (*Pause.*)   Doesn't he ?

DIANA (*laughing*).   No.   Oh, no.   Far from it.

ROGERS (*the light of understanding in his face at last*).   Oh, I see. You mean he's rather keen on you ?

DIANA.   I mustn't give him away.   It wouldn't be fair.   But if he ever talks to you about me, as he probably will, and tries to give you the impression that I'm a (*smiling*) scheming wrecker of men's lives, you needn't necessarily believe him.

ROGERS.   No—no, I won't, of course.   But I don't see why he should, you know.

DIANA (*embarrassedly—rising and sitting on* L. *end of the table*). Well, you see, Commander Rogers——

(DIANA *puts her right foot up on chair* 5 *and shows her bare leg. She says " Oh ! " and covers it up.*)

I like Alan, but I don't like him as much as perhaps he wants me to, and I suppose that makes him feel rather embittered.

ROGERS.   Ah, yes, I see.

DIANA (*gaily*).   Well, don't let's talk any more about it, because it's not a very pleasant subject.   Tell me about yourself. Tell me about the Navy. I'm always thrilled to death by anything to do with the sea.

ROGERS. Really, that's splendid.

(*There is a pause.*)

DIANA. It must be a wonderful life.

ROGERS. Yes, it's a pretty good life on the whole.

DIANA. Marvellously interesting, I should think.

ROGERS. Yes, pretty interesting.

DIANA. I bet you've had any amount of wildly exciting experiences.

ROGERS. Oh, well, you know, things have a way of happening in the Navy.

DIANA. Yes, I'm sure they have. (*Pause.*) You naval people never talk about yourselves, do you ?

ROGERS. Well, you know, silent service and all that.

DIANA (*kneeling on chair* 5 *and facing* ROGERS). Yes, I know, but I do hope you're not going to be too silent with me, because, honestly, I am so terribly interested.

ROGERS (*smiling*). I'll try not to be too silent, then.

(ROGERS *crosses down* C. *to below seat* 8. DIANA *follows him.*)

DIANA (*after a pause*). What are you doing this morning ?

ROGERS. Nothing special, why ?

DIANA. How would you like to have a look round the town ?

(JACQUELINE *enters down* L.)

JACQUELINE. Hasn't Kit come down yet ?

ROGERS. Oh, I'd love to.

DIANA. Good. I'll go and get dressed and we'll go for a little stroll.

(JACQUELINE *pours out milk and coffee for* KIT.)

ROGERS. But isn't it rather a bore for you ?

DIANA. No, of course not. I'd love it. (*She goes to the door up* L.)

JACQUELINE. Diana.

DIANA. Yes ?

JACQUELINE. If you're going past Kit's room you might give him this. (*She hands her the cup.*)

DIANA. Right, I will. (*To* ROGERS.) Are you sure I'm not dragging you away from your work or anything ?

(JACQUELINE *exits into the kitchen.*)

ROGERS. Oh, no. That's quite all right.

(ALAN *enters up* L. *and remains standing there.*)

I haven't been given anything to do yet.

DIANA. Good. Well, I'll go and put some clothes on.

(*Turning.*) I'll meet you down here, then, in about a quarter of an hour ?

ROGERS. Right.

(ROGERS *smiles at* DIANA, *who returns the smile.* ALAN *catches his eye and he is annoyed and looks out at the French window.* DIANA *walks past* ALAN *without glancing at him and goes out.* ALAN *goes to chair 2 and sits.*)

ALAN. Going for a little constitutional, Commander ? (*He has some books in his hands. He places them on the table in front of him and opens a notebook.*)

ROGERS. Yes. (*He turns his back.*)

ALAN (*taking a fountain-pen from his pocket and unscrewing the top*). You've got a nice day for it.

(ROGERS *comes round* L. *of the table and picks up his phrase-book. There is a pause.* ALAN *writes in his notebook and begins to sing the " Lorelei."*)

(*Without looking up.*) It's a lovely song, the " Lorelei," don't you think ?

ROGERS. It *could* be.

ALAN (*continuing to write*). It's a stupid fable, anyway. I ask you, what sailor would be lured to his doom after he had been warned of his danger.

ROGERS (*turning quickly*). If you think that's funny, I don't.

(ALAN *stares at him.* KENNETH *enters through the window.*)

KENNETH. Oh, Commander Rogers, Maingot wants to see you a moment.

(*There is a pause.* ROGERS *is standing facing* ALAN. ALAN *is writing.*)

ROGERS. Right. Thank you.

(*He marches out into the garden.* KENNETH *goes to the bookcase* C. *to change his book.*)

ALAN (*after a pause*). Well, Babe, I suppose you were murdered by the old man.

KENNETH (*wearily*). More so than usual this morning.

(*Another pause.* ALAN *goes on writing.*)

ALAN (*without looking up*). Babe, I don't like your sister.

KENNETH (*coming to above chair 3 and looking over* ALAN'S *shoulder at what he is writing*). Don't you ? I thought you liked her rather a lot.

(ALAN *looks up. There is a pause.* JACQUELINE *enters from the kitchen. She has taken off her apron and the handkerchief over her hair.*)

JACQUELINE. Good morning, Kenneth. (*She crosses below the table to up* R.C.)

KENNETH. Good morning, mam'selle.

JACQUELINE. Had your lesson ?

KENNETH. Yes. I've got to do the whole damn thing again. (*He goes to the door.*) Alan, I wish to God I had your brains.

(KENNETH *exits up* L. ALAN *looks after him a moment, then goes back to his work.*)

JACQUELINE (*looking at her watch*). Kit is a monster. He's never been on time for his lesson yet. (*She goes to the window and looks out.*)

ALAN (*looking up from his work*). What have you done to your hair, Jack ?

JACQUELINE (*turning round*). Do you like it ? (*Her hair is done in the same way as* DIANA'S.)

ALAN. No, it's a mistake, Jack. You won't beat her by copying the way she does her hair.

JACQUELINE. He'll like it, Alan, I'm sure he will.

ALAN. He won't notice it.

JACQUELINE. He will, you see.

ALAN. I'll bet you five francs he doesn't.

JACQUELINE. All right. That's a bet.

ALAN. Go and change it while there's still time. Make it look hideous like it used to.

JACQUELINE (*laughing*). No, Alan.

(JACQUELINE *is on the steps at the French window up* R. *There is a pause.*)

ALAN. Poor Jack, I must find you someone else to fall in love with.

JACQUELINE. So long as you don't tell him that I adore him, I don't mind what you do.

ALAN. Anyone less half-witted than Kit would have seen it years ago.

JACQUELINE. Am I very obvious, Alan ? I don't want to bore him.

ALAN. Go and change that hair.

JACQUELINE (*coming down to* R. *of* ALAN). Do you think if Diana were out of the way I should stand a chance ?

ALAN. You're not thinking of putting her out of the way, are you ?

JACQUELINE (*smiling*). I'd do it painlessly, Alan.

ALAN. Why painlessly ?

JACQUELINE. I'm not jealous of her really, though.

ALAN. Oh, no. Not a bit.

JACQUELINE. Honestly, Alan, I wouldn't mind if she made him happy. But she doesn't. She seems to enjoy making him miserable. And now that the Commander's here it's going to be much worse. You know what I mean, don't you?

ALAN. I have an idea.

JACQUELINE. Can't we do anything about it, Alan?

ALAN. Yes. (*He rises and pushes her in front of him to* L.C.) Go and change that hair, Jack. It's the only chance.

JACQUELINE. No, I won't do anything of the sort.

(KIT *enters up* L., *dressed.*)

KIT (*walking right up to* JACQUELINE). Jack, I have something to tell you. (*To* ALAN.) Go away, Alan, this is confidential.

(ALAN *goes to the table up* R., *takes a cigarette, then comes back to his seat at chair* 2 *and sits.*)

JACQUELINE. What is it, Kit?

KIT. I haven't done that work you set me.

JACQUELINE. Oh, Kit. Why not?

KIT. Well, I took Diana to the Casino last night, and——

JACQUELINE. Kit, really——

KIT. But (*he holds up his finger*) as a great treat I'll translate you some La Bruyère this morning. Come on. (*He pulls her towards the armchair down* L.)

JACQUELINE. I set you that work specially because I thought it would interest you, and anyway you can't afford to slack off just now before your exam.

KIT (*handing her a book*). Now sit down and read your nice La Bruyère and be quiet. (*He pulls down chair* 5 *and sits.*)

(JACQUELINE *sits.*)

(*Opening his own book.*) Page one hundred and eight. Listen, Alan. You can learn a lot from hearing French beautifully translated. Chapter Four. (*Reading.*) Of the heart——

JACQUELINE. Of love.

KIT. Of love, then. (*Translating.*) There is a fragrance in pure love——

JACQUELINE. In pure friendship.

KIT (*translating*). Friendship can exist between people of different sexes——

ALAN. You don't say.

KIT. I don't. La Bruyère does. (*Translating.*) Friendship can exist between people of different sexes, quite exempt from all grossness.

JACQUELINE. Quite free from all——

ALAN. Hanky-panky.

JACQUELINE. Quite free from all unworthy thoughts.

KIT. Quite exempt from all grossness. (*Looking up.*) I know what it is. It's been bothering me all the time. (*Stooping down and looking at* Jacqueline.) You've changed your hair, haven't you, Jack ?

Jacqueline (*giving* Alan *a quick glance*). Yes, Kit, I've changed my hair.

Kit. Alan, do look at Jack. She's changed her hair.

Alan (*looking up*). So she has. Well—well—well.

Kit. I knew you'd done something to yourself. (*He studies her.*) It's queer, you know. It makes you look quite . . .

Jacqueline (*eagerly*). Quite what, Kit ?

Kit. I was going to say alluring.

(*He laughs as if he'd made a joke ;* Jacqueline *laughs too.*)

Jacqueline. You do like it, anyway, Kit ?

Kit. Yes, I do. I think it's very nice.

Jacqueline. You think I ought to keep it like this ?

(*Before* Kit *can answer,* Rogers *has appeared from the garden up* R.)

Rogers. Sorry. Maingot wants to take me now, so would one of you mind telling Diana—er—I mean Miss Lake, that we'll have to postpone our walk.

(Kit *rises to above* L. *of the table.*)

Alan. Yes, I'll tell her.

Rogers. Thank you.

(*He goes out through the window again.*)

Jacqueline (*breaking a silence*). You think I ought to keep it like this ?

Kit (*turning slowly*). Keep what ?

Jacqueline. My hair.

Kit. Oh, don't be such a bore about your hair, Jack. Yes, keep it like that. It'll get a laugh, anyway.

(*He exits up* L. Jacqueline *rises up to* L. *of the table.*)

Jacqueline. Five francs, please, Alan.

(Alan *rises and fumbles for the money.*)

Curtain.

ACT II

Scene 1

SCENE.—*Same as Act I.*

TIME.—*A fortnight later, about 2 p.m.*

Lunch is just finished. All the characters seen in Act I are still sitting at the table. MAINGOT *sits at one end,* ALAN *facing him at the other end. On* MAINGOT'S *right are* ROGERS, DIANA *and* KIT, *in that order, facing the audience. On his left are* BRIAN, KENNETH *and* JACQUELINE, *also in that order, with their backs to the audience.*

On the rise of the CURTAIN, ROGERS *is getting a dessert spoon out of the drawer at the table* L. *He returns to his seat at chair 4. Conversation is general.* ALAN *is talking to* JACQUELINE, BRIAN *to* MAINGOT, *and* ROGERS *to* DIANA. *After a few seconds, conversation lapses and* ROGERS' *voice can be heard.*

ROGERS. Oh, yes, Tuppy Jones. Yes, he's in " Belligerent." I know him quite well. Cheery cove. (*He chuckles.*) There's an amusing story about him, as a matter of fact. He got a bit tight in Portsmouth, and broke seven Belisha beacons with an air pistol.

MAINGOT (*turning politely to* ROGERS). Eh, bien, Monsieur le Commandant, voulez-vous raconter votre petite histoire en français ? Please to tell your little story in French.

ROGERS (*confused*). Oh, no, sir. That's a bit unfair. I don't know enough.

MAINGOT. You should have learnt enough, my Commander.

ROGERS. But, dash it, sir, I've only been here a few days.

MAINGOT. Two weeks, my Commander. After two weeks my pupils are usually enough advanced to tell me little stories in French.

ROGERS. Well, I'm afraid I can't tell this one, sir. It wasn't a story, anyway.

ALAN (*leaning forward malevolently*). Au contraire, monsieur, l'histoire de Monsieur le Commandant était excessivement rigolo.

MAINGOT. Bien, alors. Racontez-la vous-même.

ALAN. Il paraît qu'il connaît un type qui s'appelle Tuppy Jones. Alors ce bonhomme, se promenant un soir par les rues de Portsmouth, et ayant un peu trop bu, a brisé, à coup de pistolet à vent, sept Belisha beacons.

MAINGOT (*who has been listening attentively, his ear cupped in his hand*). Et puis ?

ALAN. C'est tout, monsieur.

MAINGOT. C'est tout ?

KIT. Vous savez que ce Tuppy Jones était d'un esprit le plus fin du monde.

MAINGOT. Oh ! Je crois bien. En même temps, je n'ai pas tout à fait compris. Qu'est-ce-que'ca veut dire " Belisha Beacons " ?

ALAN. Ah, ça c'est un peu compliqué.

BRIAN (*showing off his French*). Belisha Beacons sont des objets—— (*He stops.*)

ALAN. Qui se trouvent actuellement dans les rues de Londres——

KIT. Et qui sont dédiés au salut des passants.

MAINGOT. Ah. Des emblèmes religieux ?

ALAN. C'est ça. Des emblèmes religieux.

MAINGOT (*to* ROGERS). So one finds it funny in England to break these religious emblems with a wind pistol ?

ROGERS (*not having understood*). Well——

(MAINGOT *shrugs his shoulders sadly.*)

(*Angrily to* ALAN.) Damn you, Howard.

BRIAN. That's not fair.

ALAN. It was a very good story, I thought.

MAINGOT (*having finished his wine*). Bien, messieurs, mesdames, la session est terminée.

(*He gets up.* ROGERS *attempts to rise, but* MAINGOT *signals him to wait and stay in his seat.*)

One moment, please. I speak in English for those who cannot understand. How many of you are going to-night to the Costume Ball and great battle of flowers at the Casino ? Please hold up your hands.

(*All hold up their hands.*)

KIT (*to* ALAN). Good Lord ! Is it July the fourteenth ? I'd no idea.

MAINGOT. All of you. Good. The festivities commence at eight o'clock ; there will be no dinner 'ere. All right.

(*There is a chorus of assent.* MAINGOT *moves to the window* R. ALAN *rises.* JACQUELINE *rises and exits down* L. *into the kitchen.* MAIN-GOT *suddenly stops and turns.*)

One moment, please. I give my history lecture at two-thirty— that is to say, in twenty minutes' time. All right.

(*He exits into the garden.* DIANA *rises to above* KIT'S *chair.*)

KIT (*to* DIANA). What about a game of Japanese billiards, Diana ?

DIANA (*indicating* ROGERS). Bill's just asked me to play, Kit. I'll play you afterwards. Come on, Bill.

ROGERS (*rising*). Sorry, Neilan.

(ROGERS *and* DIANA *go out together up* R. BRIAN *has pulled out a wallet and is fumbling inside it.* ALAN *is going out through the window when* KENNETH *catches him up.*)

KENNETH. Alan, will you help me with that essay now ? You said you would.

ALAN. Oh, hell ! Can't you do it yourself ?

KENNETH. Well, I could, but it might mean missing this dance to-night and I'd hate that. Do help me, it's on Robespierre, and I know nothing about him.

ALAN. There's a chapter on him in Lavisse. Why don't you copy that out ? The old man won't notice. He'll probably say it isn't French, but still——

(*He goes out.*)

KENNETH (*following him*). Alan, be a sportsman.

ALAN (*off*). Nothing I should hate more.

KENNETH. Oh, hell ! (*He turns sadly and goes past* KIT *to the door at the back up* L.)

KIT (*moodily*). What Alan wants is a good kick in the pants.

KENNETH (*at the door*). Oh, I don't know.

(*He goes out.* BRIAN *puts his wallet back in his pocket, rises and goes to above chair 5.*)

BRIAN. I say, old boy, I suppose you couldn't lend me fifty francs, could you ?

KIT. No, I couldn't. At any rate, not until you've paid me back that hundred you owe me.

BRIAN. Ah, I see your point. (*Cheerfully.*) Well, old boy, no ill feelings. I'll have to put off Chi-Chi for to-night, that's all.

KIT. You weren't thinking of taking her to this thing at the Casino, were you ?

BRIAN. Yes.

KIT. What do you think Maingot would have said if he'd seen her ?

BRIAN. That would have been all right. I told him I was taking the daughter of the British Consul.

KIT. But she doesn't exactly look like the daughter of the British Consul, does she ?

BRIAN. Well, after all, it's fancy dress. It's just possible the daughter of the British Consul might go dressed as Nana of the Boulevards. Still, I admit that if he'd actually met her he might have found it odd that the only English she knew was, " I love you, Big Boy."

KIT. How do you manage to talk to her, then ?

BRIAN. Oh, we get along, old boy, we get along. (*Going to the window.*) You couldn't make it thirty francs, I suppose ?

KIT. No, and I don't suppose Chi-Chi could either.

BRIAN. Oh, well, you may be right. I'd better pop round in the car and tell her I won't be there to-night.

KIT (*rising and moving to the window* R.). Oh, listen, Brian, if you want someone to take, why don't you take Jack?

BRIAN. Isn't anyone taking her?

KIT. Yes, I'm supposed to be, but——

BRIAN (*surprised*). You, old boy? What about Diana?

KIT. Oh, she's being taken by the Commander.

BRIAN. Oh!

(*There is a pause.*)

As a matter of fact, I don't think I'll go at all. I don't fancy myself at a battle of flowers.

KIT. Nor do I, if it comes to that.

BRIAN. Oh, I don't know. I think you'd hurl a prettier bloom than I would. Well, so long.

(*He goes out through the window.* KIT *stands for a moment looking after him, then moves down to the table* R. *and picks up a magazine.* DIANA *is heard to laugh outside.* KIT *throws the magazine across the room in a temper.* JACQUELINE *and* MARIANNE *enters from down* L., *and* MARIANNE *picks up the magazine and puts it on the table* L. *The two girls have a tray each for clearing the table. The ferocious din of a sports car tuning up comes through the window.* KIT *turns angrily.*)

KIT (*shouting through the window*). Must you make all that noise?

BRIAN (*off, coming faintly above the din*). Can't hear, old boy.

(*The noise lessens as the car moves off down the street.* JACQUELINE *starts to clear from below* R. *of the table;* MARIANNE *goes to* L. *end of the table.*)

KIT (*turning*). God knows why Brian finds it necessary to have a car that sounds like—like five dictators all talking at once. (*He takes another magazine and his notebook from the table* R. *and sits in the armchair down* R.)

JACQUELINE (*helping* MARIANNE *clear*). It goes with his character, Kit. He'd think it was effeminate to have a car that was possible to sit in without getting cramp and that didn't deafen one.

KIT. I wonder what it's like to be as hearty as Brian?

JACQUELINE. Awful, I should think.

KIT. No, I should think very pleasant. Have you ever seen Brian bad-tempered?

JACQUELINE. No, but then I think he's too stupid to be bad-tempered.

KIT. It doesn't follow. Cats and dogs are bad-tempered, sometimes. No, Brian may be stupid but he's right-minded. He's solved the problem of living better than any of us.

(MARIANNE *goes out down* L. *with a loaded tray.* KIT *rises and goes and looks through the window up* R.)

It seems a simple solution, too. All it needs, apparently, is the occasional outlay of fifty francs. I wish I could do the same.

JACQUELINE. I expect you could if you tried.

KIT. I have tried. Often. Does that shock you ? (*He comes down to chair* 1.)

JACQUELINE. Why should it ?

KIT. I just wondered.

JACQUELINE. I'm a woman of the world.

KIT (*smiling*). That's the last thing you are. (*He sits at the table, in chair* 2.) But I'll tell you this, Jack. I like you so much that it's sometimes quite an effort to remember that you're a woman at all.

JACQUELINE. Oh !

(KIT *picks up the sugar caster and handles it.*)

I thought you liked women.

KIT. I don't think one likes women, does one ? One loves them sometimes, but that's a different thing altogether. Still, I like you. That's what's so odd.

JACQUELINE (*brightly, taking the caster from him*). Thank you, Kit. I like you too.

KIT. Good. That's nice for both of us, isn't it ? (*He returns his gaze to the window.*)

(JACQUELINE *takes the tray and almost drops it on the table* L.)

Clumsy !

JACQUELINE. Have you found anything to wear to-night ? (*She returns to the table, takes off the cloth and starts to fold it.*)

KIT (*rising*). Supposing I didn't go, would you mind ? (*He moves to above chair* 3.)

JACQUELINE (*giving* KIT *the end of the cloth to fold*). Well, I have been rather looking forward to to-night.

KIT. Alan could take you. He's a better dancer than I am.

JACQUELINE (*after a pause*). Why don't you wear that Greek dress of my brother's ?

KIT. Jack, you know, I don't think I could cope with a battle of flowers. (*He turns and meets her eyes.*)

JACQUELINE. Oh, Kit !

KIT. Well, could I get into this dress of your brother's ?

JACQUELINE. Yes, easily. It may be a bit tight.

(ALAN *comes in through the window to above chair* 1.)

KIT. That reminds me. I hope there'll be plenty to drink at this affair.

ALAN (*morosely*). There's nothing else for it. I shall have to murder that man.

JACQUELINE. Who ?
ALAN. The Commander.

(JACQUELINE *exits down* L. *with the tray and cloth.*)

KIT (*sitting in chair* 3). Surely that's my privilege, isn't it ?
ALAN. I've just been watching him play Japanese billiards with Diana. Now you would think, wouldn't you, that Japanese billiards was a fairly simple game. You either roll wooden balls into holes or you don't. That should be the end of it. But as played by the Commander it becomes a sort of naval battle. (*He lights a cigarette from his case.*) Every shot he makes is either a plunging salvo or a blasting broadside or a direct hit amidships. (*He sits in the armchair down* R.)
KIT. At least he has the excuse that it amuses Diana.

(JACQUELINE *re-enters with two clean ashtrays, which she puts on the table* C. *She then moves chair* 4 *up to* L. *of the bookcase and chair* 2 *up to* R. *of the bookcase, then goes and looks out of the window up* R.)

Will you explain to me, Alan, as an impartial observer, how she can bear to be more than two minutes in that man's company ?
ALAN. Certainly. He's in the process of falling in love with her.
KIT. Yes, that's obvious, but——
ALAN. When one hooks a salmon one has to spend a certain amount of time playing it. If one doesn't, it escapes.
KIT. Is that meant to be funny ?
ALAN. Of course, when the salmon is landed all that's necessary is an occasional kick to prevent it slipping back into the water.
KIT (*angrily*). Don't be a damned fool.
ALAN. To-morrow a certain Lord Heybrook is arriving. Diana is naturally rather anxious to bring the Commander to the gaff as quickly as possible, so that she can have two nice fat fish gasping and squirming about on the bank before she starts to fish for what'll be the best catch of all of you, if she can bring it off.

(*There is a pause.* KIT *suddenly bursts out laughing.*)

KIT. No wonder you can't get anyone to take your novel.
ALAN (*hurt*). I can't quite see what my novel has got to do with the machinations of a scalp-hunter.
KIT (*rising and walking over to* ALAN). Listen, Alan. One more crack like that——
JACQUELINE (*hurriedly, coming down to between* KIT *and* ALAN). Kit's quite right. You shouldn't say things like that.
KIT (*turning to her savagely*). What do you know about it, anyway ?
JACQUELINE. Nothing, only——
KIT. Well, please go away. This is between Alan and me.
JACQUELINE. Oh, I'm sorry.

(*She turns and goes into the garden.*)

KIT. Now. Will you please understand this. I am in love with Diana, and Diana is in love with me. Now that's not too hard for you to grasp, is it, because I'll repeat it again slowly if you like ?

ALAN (*genially*). No, no. I've read about that sort of thing in books. The Commander of course is just an old friend who's known her since she was so high. (*He denotes height with his hand.*)

KIT. The Commander's in love with her, but you can't blame Diana for that.

ALAN. Of course I don't. It was a very smart piece of work on her part.

KIT (*turning and walking to C., swallowing his anger*). She's too kind-hearted to tell him to go to hell——

ALAN. I suppose it's because she's so kind-hearted that she calls him " darling," and plays these peculiar games with him all over the place.

(KIT *turns to face him and puts his foot on the table-bench.*)

KIT. I called you an impartial observer a moment ago. Well, you're not. I believe you're in love with Diana yourself.

ALAN. My dear Kit ! As a matter of fact, I admit it's quite possible I shall end by marrying her.

KIT. You'll what ?

ALAN. But that'll only be—to take another sporting metaphor —like the stag who turns at bay through sheer exhaustion at being hunted.

(*There is a pause.*)

KIT (*aggressively, going up to him*). God ! Alan, I've a good mind to——

ALAN. I shouldn't. It'd make us both look rather silly.

(DIANA *and* ROGERS *are heard off in the garden.*)

Besides, you know how strongly I disapprove of fighting over a woman.

(DIANA *appears at the window,* ROGERS *following.*)

ROGERS (*coming in through the window*). Well, of course, there was only one thing to do. So I gave the order—all hands on deck. (*He stops at sight of* KIT *and* ALAN.)

ALAN. And did they come ?

ROGERS (*ignoring* ALAN--*to* DIANA). Let's go out in the garden, Diana.

DIANA. It's so hot, Bill. Let's stay here.

(KIT *goes to* L. *of* DIANA.)

KIT. Aren't you going to play me a game of Japanese billiards, Diana ?

DIANA. You don't mind, do you, Kit ? I'm quite exhausted, as a matter of fact.

KIT (*furious*). Oh no. I don't mind a bit.

(*He goes out into the garden. There is a pause.* ALAN *begins to hum the " Lorelei."* ROGERS *walks towards the door up* L.)

ALAN (*rising*). Don't leave us, Commander. If one of us has to go, let it be myself.

(ROGERS *stops.* ALAN *walks to the door up* L. DIANA *sits in the armchair down* R.)

I shall go aloft.

(*He goes out up* L.)

ROGERS. Silly young fool. I'd like to have him in my ship. Do him all the good in the world.

DIANA. Yes. It might knock some of the conceit out of him.

ROGERS. Yes. (*He pulls out chair* 1 *and sits by* DIANA.) Has he been—bothering you at all lately ?

DIANA (*with a gesture of resignation*). Oh, well. I'm awfully sorry for him, you know.

ROGERS. I find it hard to understand you sometimes, Diana. At least, I think I do understand you, but if you don't mind me saying it, I think you're too kind-hearted—far too kind-hearted.

DIANA (*with a sigh*). Yes, I think I am.

ROGERS. For instance—I can't understand why you don't tell Kit.

DIANA (*rising and taking* ROGERS' *hand*). Oh, Bill, please——

ROGERS. I'm sorry to keep on at you about it, Diana, but you don't know how much I resent him behaving as if you were still in love with him.

DIANA. But I can't tell him—not yet, anyway. (*Gently.*) Surely you must see how cruel that would be ?

ROGERS. This is a case where you must be cruel only to be kind.

DIANA. Yes, Bill, that's true. Terribly true. (*She moves to above his chair.*) But you know, cruelty is something that's physically impossible to me. I'm the sort of person who's miserable if I tread on a snail.

ROGERS. You must tell him, Diana. Otherwise it's so unfair on him. Tell him now.

DIANA (*quickly*). No, not now.

ROGERS. Well, this evening.

DIANA (*coming down in front of the table*). Well, I'll try. It's a terribly hard thing to do. It's like—it's like kicking someone when he's down.

(ROGERS *rises, comes to her and puts an arm round her.*)

ROGERS. I know, old girl, it's a rotten thing to have to do.

(*Both sit on the bench.*)

Poor little girl, you mustn't think I don't sympathize with you, you know.

DIANA (*laying her head on his chest*). Oh, Bill, I do feel such a beast.

ROGERS. Yes, yes, of course. But these things happen, you know.

DIANA. I can't understand it even yet. I loved Kit—at least I thought I did, and then you happened—and—and—— (*Taking her head off his shoulder.*) Oh, Bill, do you do this to all the women you meet?

ROGERS. Er—do what?

DIANA. Sweep them off their feet so that they forget everything in the world except you.

ROGERS. Diana, will you give me a truthful answer to a question I'm going to ask you?

DIANA. Yes, of course, Bill.

ROGERS. Is your feeling for me mere—infatuation, or do you really really love me?

DIANA. Oh, you know I do, Bill.

ROGERS. Oh, darling. And you really don't love Kit any more?

DIANA. I'm still fond of him.

ROGERS. But you don't love him?

DIANA. No, Bill, I don't love him.

(JACQUELINE *comes in through the window.* ROGERS, *his back to her, doesn't see her.* DIANA *breaks away.*)

ROGERS. And you will tell him so?

DIANA. Hullo, Jacqueline.

JACQUELINE. Hullo, Diana. Rather warm, isn't it?

(*She walks across the room and into the kitchen.* ROGERS *and* DIANA *rise.*)

DIANA (*alarmed*). You don't think she saw anything, do you?

ROGERS. I don't know.

(ROGERS *puts his foot on the bench.*)

DIANA. She may have been standing outside the window the whole time. I wouldn't put it past her.

ROGERS. What does it matter, anyway? Everyone will know soon enough.

DIANA (*thoughtfully*). She's the sort of girl who'll talk.

ROGERS. Let her.

DIANA (*turning to him and sitting on the bench again*). Bill, you don't understand. Our feelings for each other are too sacred to be soiled by vulgar gossip.

ROGERS (*taking her hand*). Yes. But, darling, we can't go on keeping it a secret for ever.

DIANA. Not for ever. But don't you find it thrilling to have such a lovely secret just between us and no one else ? After all, it's our love. Why should others know about it and bandy it about ?

ROGERS. Yes, I know, but——

(KIT *comes in through the window.* ROGERS *releases* DIANA'S *hand.* KIT *glances moodily at* DIANA *and* ROGERS, *picks up a paper from the table* R., *throws himself into the armchair down* R. *and begins to read.* ROGERS *points significantly at him and frames the words* " Tell him now " *in his mouth.* DIANA *shakes her head violently.* ROGERS *nods his head urgently.* KIT *looks up.* DIANA *rises.*)

DIANA (*hurriedly*). You people have got a lecture now, haven't you ?

KIT. In about five minutes.

DIANA. Oh ! (*Going to the window up* R.) Then I think I'll go for a little walk by myself. We'll have our bathe about four, don't you think, Bill ?

ROGERS. Right. (*He moves up* L.)

(DIANA *goes out. There is a pause.* ROGERS *strolls to chair* 1, *puts a foot on it and takes out a cigarette.*)

(*Breezily.*) Well, Neilan, how's the world treating you these days ?

KIT. Bloodily.

ROGERS. I'm sorry to hear that. What's the trouble ?

KIT. Everything. (*He takes up the paper.*)

ROGERS (*after a pause*). This show to-night at the Casino ought to be rather cheery, don't you think ?

(KIT *lowers his paper, looks at him, and raises it again.*)

Who are you taking ?

KIT (*into the paper*). Jacqueline.

ROGERS. Jacqueline ?

KIT (*loudly*). Yes, Jacqueline.

ROGERS. Oh. (*Cheerfully, as he goes to the table up* R. *for a match.*) That's a charming girl, I think. Clever. Amusing. Pretty. She'll make somebody a fine wife.

(KIT *emits a kind of snort.*)

She's what the French call a sympathetic person.

KIT. Do they ? I didn't know.

ROGERS. Oh, they do. Much nicer than most modern girls. Take some of these English girls, for instance——

KIT. You take them. I want to read.*

(*He turns his back.* ROGERS, *annoyed, shrugs his shoulders, then*

goes to the bookcase and takes out his notebook. BRIAN'S *voice can
be heard in the garden singing "Somebody stole my girl.")*

(*Shouting.*) Blast you, Brian!

BRIAN (*appearing at the window*). What's the matter, old boy !
Don't you like my voice ?

KIT. No; and I don't like that song.

BRIAN. "Somebody stole my girl"? Why, it's a—— (*He
looks from* KIT *to* ROGERS.) Perhaps you're right. It's not one of
my better efforts. (*He puts a parcel on the table.*) This has just
come for Alan. It feels suspiciously like his novel. You won't
believe it, but I used to sing in my school choir. Only because I
was in the rugger fifteen, I admit. (*He goes to the bookcase and takes
out his notebook.*) What's the old boy lecturing on to-day ?

KIT. The Near East, I suppose. He didn't finish it yesterday.

BRIAN. Good Lord ! (*He comes down to* L. *of* KIT.) Was it the
Near East yesterday ? I thought it was the Franco-Prussian War.

KIT. You must get a lot of value out of these lectures.

BRIAN. Well, I only understood one word in a hundred.

ROGERS. It's rather the same in my case. (*He takes chair 2 from*
R. *of bookcase, brings it to above* R. *end of the table and sits.*)

BRIAN. Give me your notes in case the old boy has the imper-
tinence to ask me a question.

(*He takes* KIT'S *notes, sits at seat 6, and starts to read them.* ALAN
    comes in through the door up L., *followed by* KENNETH. *Both
    have books.*)

ALAN (*going to chair 1 and picking up the parcel*). Ah, I see the
novel has come home to father again.

(KENNETH *comes to upstage* L. *end of table and sits on it.*)

BRIAN. Open it, old boy. There may be a marvellous letter
inside.

ALAN. There'll be a letter all right. But I don't need to read it.
(*He sits down at the table and pushes the parcel away.*)

BRIAN. Bad luck, old boy.

(KENNETH *grabs the parcel and unties the string.*)

You mustn't give up hope yet, though. First novels are always
refused hundreds of times. I know a bloke who's been writing
novels and plays and things all his life. He's fifty now, and he's
still hoping to get something accepted.

ALAN. Thank you, Brian. That's very comforting.

(KENNETH *has extracted a letter from the parcel and is reading it.*)

ROGERS (*amicably*). Will you let me read it sometime ?
ALAN (*pleased*). Would you like to ?

(KENNETH *gives* ALAN *the letter.*)

I'm afraid you'd hate it. (*He glances through the letter and throws .it on the table.*)

ROGERS. Why ? What's it about ?

ALAN. It's about two young men who take a vow to desert their country instantly in the case of war and to go and live on a farm in Central Africa.

ROGERS (*uncomfortably*). Oh !

ALAN. War breaks out and they go. One of them takes his wife. They go, not because they are any more afraid to fight than the next man, but because they believe violence in any circumstances to be a crime and that, if the world goes mad, it's their duty to remain sane.

ROGERS. I see. Conchies.

(ALAN *turns and looks at* KIT.)

ALAN. Yes. Conchies. When they get to their farm one of them makes love to the other's wife and they fight over her.

ROGERS. Ah ! That's a good point.

ALAN. But in fighting for her they are perfectly aware that the motive that made them do it is as vile as the impulse they feel to go back and fight for their country. (*He rises and walks below the table to* L. *of chair* 5.) In both cases they are letting their passions get the better of their reason—becoming animals instead of men.

ROGERS. But that's nonsense. If a man fights for his country or his wife he's—well, he's a man and not a damned conchie.

ALAN (*advancing towards* ROGERS). The characters in my book have the honesty not to rationalize the animal instinct to fight, into something noble like patriotism or manliness. They admit that it's an ignoble instinct—something to be ashamed of.

ROGERS (*heated*). Ashamed of ! Crikey !

ALAN. But they also admit that their reason isn't strong enough to stand out against this ignoble instinct, so they go back and fight. (*He moves to the window up* R.)

ROGERS. Ah ! That's more like it. So they were proved wrong in the end.

ALAN. Their ideal wasn't proved wrong because they were unable to live up to it. That's the point of the book.

KIT (*from his corner, morosely*). What's the use of an ideal if you can't live up to it ?

ALAN (*coming down to* L. *of* KIT). In a hundred years' time men may be able to live up to our ideals even if they can't live up to their own.

KENNETH (*excitedly*). That's it. Progress.

KIT. Progress my fanny.

ROGERS. But look here, are you a pacifist and all that ?

ALAN (*moving to* R. *of the table* C.). I am a pacifist and all that.

ROGERS. And you're going into the diplomatic.

ALAN. Your surprise is a damning criticism of the diplomatic. Anyway, it's not my fault. My father's an ambassador.

ROGERS. Still, I mean to say—— Look here, supposing some rotter came along and stole your best girl, wouldn't you fight him ?

KIT (*throwing down his paper and looking up*). You'd better ask me that question, hadn't you ?

ROGERS (*swinging round*). What the devil do you mean ?

KIT (*rising to* R.C.). And the answer would be yes.

ROGERS (*with heavy sarcasm—rising*). That's very interesting, I'm sure.

ALAN (*enjoying himself*). By the way, I forgot to tell you, in my novel, when the two men go back to fight for their country they leave the woman in Central Africa. (*He faces* ROGERS.) You see, after fighting over her they come to the conclusion that she's a bitch. It would have been so much better, don't you think, if they had discovered that sooner ?

KIT. All right, you asked for it.

(*He turns* ALAN *towards him roughly and raises his arm to hit him.* ALAN *grapples with him and holds him.*)

ALAN. Don't be a damned fool.

(ROGERS *seizes* ALAN *from behind and throws him into chair* 3.)

KIT (*turning furiously on* ROGERS). What the hell do you think you're doing ?

KENNETH. Yes. What the hell do you think you're doing ?

(KIT *aims a blow at* ROGERS, *who dodges it, overturning a chair.* KENNETH *also runs in to attack* ROGERS. BRIAN, *also running in, tries to restrain both* KENNETH *and* KIT.)

BRIAN. Shut up, you damned lot of fools. (*Shouting.*) Kit, Babe, show some sense, for God's sake ! (*Suddenly.*) Look out ! Maingot !

(ALAN *gets up and is about to go for* ROGERS *when* MAINGOT *comes in from the garden, carrying a large notebook under his arm.* ROGERS *and* ALAN *stand glaring at each other.*)

MAINGOT. Alors, asseyez-vous, messieurs.

(*All become silent and they return to their chairs :* ALAN 1, ROGERS 2, KENNETH 3, BRIAN 6 *and* KIT 8. MAINGOT *sits in chair* 5.)

Le subjet cet après-midi sera la crise de mille huit cent quarante en Turquie.

(ALAN *and* ROGERS *are still glaring at each other.*)

Or la dernière fois je vous ai expliqué comment le gouverneur Ottoman d'Egypte, Mehemet Ali, s'était battu contre son souverain, le Sultan de Turquie. Constatons donc que la chute du Sultanat . . .

CURTAIN.

SCENE 2

SCENE.—*The same.*

TIME.—*About six hours later.*

(*For slight alterations to set see Property Plot.*)

DIANA *is discovered sitting in the armchair down* R., *her feet up on the stool. She is smoking a cigarette and is reading a magazine. Almost immediately* JACQUELINE *enters up* L. *and comes* C. *She is dressed in a Bavarian costume.*

JACQUELINE. Hullo! Aren't you getting dressed?

DIANA (*turning her head, then getting up and examining* JACQUELINE). Darling, you look too lovely.

JACQUELINE. Do you like it?

DIANA. I adore it. I think it's sweet. (*She continues her examination.*) If I were you, dear, I'd wear that hat just a little more on the back of the head. Look, I'll show you. (*She arranges* JACQUELINE'S *hat.*) No, that's not quite right. I wonder if it'd look better without a hat at all. (*She removes the hat.*) No, you must wear a hat.

JACQUELINE. I suppose my hair's wrong.

DIANA. Well, it isn't quite Bavarian, is it, darling? Very nice, of course. (*Pulling* JACQUELINE'S *dress about.*) There's something wrong here. It shouldn't stick out like that. Ah. That's it. I see what's wrong. Just a minute. I'll fix it. (*She kneels down and begins to rearrange the dress.*)

JACQUELINE. Diana. (*Pause.*) I've got something to say to you. Do you mind if I say it now?

DIANA. Of course not. (*Tugging the dress.*) Oh, Lord, there's a bit of braid coming off here.

JACQUELINE. Oh!

DIANA. I'll fix it for you.

JACQUELINE. If you look in that basket over there, you'll find a needle and thread. (*She points to a work-basket which is on the under shelf of the table* L. *of the armchair down* R.)

DIANA. Right. (*She goes to the basket.*)

JACQUELINE. But you needn't trouble——

DIANA (*extracting needle and thread*). That's all right. It's no trouble. I enjoy doing this sort of thing. (*She goes up to the window to thread the needle.*) Well, what was it you wanted to say to me?

JACQUELINE. I overheard your conversation with the Commander this afternoon.

DIANA (*coming back to* JACQUELINE). All of it, or just a part of it?

JACQUELINE. I heard you say that you were in love with the Commander and that you didn't love Kit.

DIANA. Oh! (*Kneeling at* JACQUELINE'S *feet.*) Now, scream if I prick you, won't you? (*She begins to sew.*) Is that what you wanted to tell me?

JACQUELINE. I wanted to know if you were going to tell Kit that you didn't love him.

DIANA (*sewing industriously*). Why ?

JACQUELINE. Because if you don't tell him, I will.

DIANA (*after a slight pause*). My poor Jacqueline, I never knew you felt like that about Kit.

JACQUELINE. Yes, you did. You've known for some time, and you've had a lot of fun out of it.

DIANA. Well, I wish you the best of luck.

JACQUELINE. Thank you. (*Starting.*) Ow !

DIANA. Sorry, darling, did I prick you ?

JACQUELINE. Are you going to tell him ?

DIANA. No—I don't think so.

JACQUELINE. I shall, then.

DIANA. My dear, I think that would be very silly. He won't believe you, it'll make him very unhappy, and, worst of all, he'll be furious with you.

JACQUELINE (*thoughtfully*). Yes, that's true, I suppose.

DIANA (*biting off the thread and standing up*). There. How's that ?

JACQUELINE. Thank you so much. That's splendid.

(DIANA *returns the needle to the basket.*)

So you won't leave Kit alone ?   (*She goes to the sofa and sits on the* L. *arm.*)

DIANA. Now, let's be honest, for a moment. Don't let's talk about love and things like that, but just plain facts. You and I both want the same man.

JACQUELINE. But you don't——

DIANA. Oh, yes, I do.

JACQUELINE. But what about the Commander ?

DIANA. I want him too. (*She comes to* R. *end of the sofa and sits.*) Don't look shocked, darling. You see, I'm not like you. You're clever—you can talk intelligently, and you're nice.

JACQUELINE. That's a horrid word.

DIANA. Now I'm not nice. I'm not clever and I can't talk intelligently. There's only one thing I've got, and I don't think you'll deny it. I have got a sort of gift for making men fall in love with me.

JACQUELINE. Oh, no. I don't deny that at all.

DIANA. Thank you, darling. I didn't think you would. Well, now, you have been sent into the world with lots of gifts, and you make use of them. Well, what about me, with just my one gift ? I must use that too, mustn't I ?

JACQUELINE. Well, what you call my gifts are at any rate social. Yours are definitely anti-social.

DIANA. Oh, I can't be bothered with all that. The fact remains that having men in love with me is my whole life. It's hard for

you to understand, I know. You see, you're the sort of person
that people like. Nobody likes me.

JACQUELINE. Oh, I wish you wouldn't keep harping on that.
I wouldn't mind if everybody hated me, provided Kit loved me.

DIANA. You can't have it both ways, darling. Kit looks on
you as a very nice person.

JACQUELINE (*with sudden anger*). Oh, God ! what I'd give to be
anything but nice. (*She rises and goes up* R. *to the window*.)

DIANA (*putting her feet up on the sofa*). In a way, you know, I
envy you. It must be very pleasant to be able to make friends with
people.

JACQUELINE. You could be friends with Kit if you were honest
with him.

DIANA. Darling ! And I called you intelligent ! Kit despises
me. If he didn't love me he'd loathe me. That's why I can't let
him go.

JACQUELINE (*pleadingly, coming to* R. *of* DIANA). Oh, Diana, I
do see your point of view. I do see that you must have men in
love with you, but couldn't you, please, couldn't you make the
Commander do ?

DIANA. No—I always act on the principle that there's safety
in numbers.

JACQUELINE. Well, there's this Lord Heybrook arriving to-
morrow. Supposing I let you have the Commander and him.

DIANA. No, darling. I'm sorry. I'd do anything else for you,
but if you want Kit, you must win him in fair fight.

JACQUELINE. You know I don't stand a chance against you.

DIANA. To be perfectly honest, I don't think you do.

JACQUELINE. I only hope you make some awful blunder, so that
he finds out the game you're playing.

DIANA (*with dignity*). I don't make blunders.

(JACQUELINE *turns away*.)

(*Rising and crossing to the table* R.) He's taking you to the Casino
to-night, isn't he ?

JACQUELINE (*sitting on the* L. *arm of the sofa and putting her hat
on the sofa*). Yes, but he's so furious because you're going with
the Commander that he'll give me the most dreadful evening.

DIANA. That's all right. I'm not going. I don't feel like it,
as a matter of fact.

JACQUELINE. But have you told the Commander ?

DIANA (*picking up a magazine*). Yes, he's furious, poor poppet,
but it's very good for him.

JACQUELINE (*after a pause*). I wonder if you realize the trouble
you cause ? You know there was a fight about you this afternoon ?

DIANA. Yes. I hear Alan was in it. That's *very* interesting.

(DIANA *smiles.* KIT'S *voice is heard off, calling,* " Jack, where are
you ? " JACQUELINE *turns to* DIANA *in sudden fright.*)

JACQUELINE (*rising and crossing to* R. *of the sofa*). Does Kit know you're not going to-night ?

(KIT *comes in through the door up* L. *His lower half is enclosed in the frilly skirt of a Greek Evzone, beneath which can be seen an ordinary pair of socks with suspenders. In addition, he wears a cricket shirt and tie. He carries the tunic over his arm.*)

KIT (*coming down* L.C.). Jack, I can't get into this damned coat.

(DIANA *bursts into a shriek of laughter.*)

DIANA. Kit, you look angelic ! I wish you could see yourself.

(KIT *crosses to between* DIANA *and* JACQUELINE.)

KIT. You shut up.

(DIANA *sits in the armchair down* R. KIT *scowls at her.*)

JACQUELINE. I told you it might be rather a tight fit.
KIT. But it's miles too small. Your brother must be a pigmy.
JACQUELINE. Take that shirt off and then try.
KIT. Jack, would you mind terribly if I didn't come ? I can't go dressed as an inebriated danseuse.

(DIANA *shrieks with laughter again.*)

JACQUELINE. Don't be silly, Kit. It's going to look lovely.
KIT. Honestly, though, I don't think I'll come. You wouldn't mind ?
JACQUELINE. I'd mind—awfully.
KIT. Alan's not going. I don't think I can face it, really. I've asked Babe if he'll take you and he says he'd love to. (*Turning to* DIANA—*off-handedly.*) I hear you're not going, Diana.
DIANA. No. I feel rather like you about it.
KIT (*to* DIANA). You know, they have dancing in the streets to-night. We might get rid of the others later and go out and join in the general whoopee—what do you say ?

(JACQUELINE *goes to* L. *of the sofa.*)

DIANA. Yes, that's a lovely idea, Kit.
KIT (*turning to* JACQUELINE). I'm awfully sorry, Jack, but honestly——
JACQUELINE. It's all right. I'll have a lovely time with Kenneth.

(*She goes out quickly through the door up* L.)

KIT. She seems rather odd. You don't think she minds, do you ?
DIANA. Well, how on earth should I know ?

(KIT *puts the tunic on* R. *end of the sofa and goes to* DIANA.)

KIT. Darling, if we go out to-night, you will get rid of the

Commander, won't you ?   If he comes I won't be answerable for the consequences.

DIANA.   He's not so easy to get rid of.   He clings like a limpet. Still, I'll do my best.

KIT.   I can't understand why you don't just tell him to go to hell.

DIANA (*gently*).   That'd be a little—cruel, wouldn't it, Kit ?

KIT.   As someone said once, why not be cruel only to be kind ?

DIANA.   Yes, that's true, that's terribly true ; but, you know, Kit, cruelty is something that's physically impossible to me.   I'm the sort of person who's miserable if I tread on a snail.

KIT.   But can't you see, darling, it's unfair on him to let him go on thinking he's got a hope ?

DIANA.   Poor old Bill.   Oh, well, darling, come and give me a kiss and say you love me.

(ROGERS *enters from up* L.)

KIT.   With pleasure. (*He kisses her.*)   I love you.

ROGERS (*to* KIT).   What the devil do you think you're doing ?

KIT.   I'll give you three guesses.

ROGERS.   I've had enough of this.   I'm going to give this young puppy a good hiding.

DIANA (*rising and crossing between them*).   Don't be silly, Bill.

ROGERS.   Out of the way, Diana.

KIT.   Do what the Commander says, Diana.

DIANA (*still separating them*).   You're both quite mad.

(MAINGOT *comes in through the door up* L., *dressed in Scottish Highland costume.* BRIAN *and* ALAN *follow, gazing at him with rapture.* KIT *and* ROGERS *and* DIANA *break apart.*)

ALAN (*above* L. *end of the sofa, clasping his hands in admiration*). Mais c'est exquis, monsieur.   Parfait.

MAINGOT (C.).   N'est-ce pas que c'est beau ?   Je l'ai choisi moi-même.   Ça me va bien, hein ?

ALAN.   C'est tout ce qu'il y a de plus chic.

BRIAN (*above* R. *end of the sofa*).   Vous ne pouvez pas dire la différence entre vous et un réel Highlander.

MAINGOT.   Mais oui.   Ça—c'est un véritable costume écossais.

DIANA.   Oh, yes, that is formidable.

MAINGOT (*crossing to* DIANA).   Vous croyez ?   Et aussi je connais quelques pas du can-can écossais.

ALAN.   Amusez-vous bien, monsieur.

MAINGOT (*going to the window* R.).   Merci.

BRIAN.   J'espère que vous baiserez beaucoup de dames, monsieur.

MAINGOT (*turning at the window*).   Hein ?   Qu'est qu'il dit, ce garçon là ?

BRIAN.   Ai-je dit quelquechose ?

MAINGOT.   Une bétise, monsieur.   On ne dit jamais baiser— embrasser.   Faut pas me donner des idées.

(*He goes out up* R. ALAN, BRIAN *and* DIANA *go to the window to watch him go down the street.* KIT *and* ROGERS *stand looking at each other rather sheepishly.*)

ALAN. My God! What *does* he look like?
DIANA. He looks perfectly sweet.

(JACQUELINE *comes in up* L., *followed by* KENNETH, *in sailor costume.* KIT *picks up the tunic from the sofa and goes up* L.)

BRIAN. Your father's just gone off, Jack. If you hurry you can catch him.
JACQUELINE. Right. (*Gaily.*) Good-bye, everyone. You're all fools not to be coming. We're going to have a lovely time. (*She picks up her hat from the sofa and crosses to the window up* R.)
KENNETH. Alan, do change your mind and come.
ALAN. No, thank you, Babe—have a good time.

(JACQUELINE *exits with* KENNETH *up* R.)

Well, I'm going to have a drink. Anyone coming with me?
BRIAN. I'm ahead of you, old boy.

(*He exits up* R.)

DIANA. Yes, I'm coming.
ALAN. I suppose that means I'll have to pay for both of you.
DIANA. Yes, it does!

(*She goes out after* BRIAN.)

ALAN. Are you two coming?

(ROGERS *and* KIT *look at each other and then shake their heads.*)

ROGERS. }
KIT. } No.
ALAN. Oh, no; I see you're going to have a musical evening!

(*He exits through the window up* R.)

KIT. Now we can have our little talk. (*He puts the tunic on* L. *end of the sofa.*)
ROGERS. I don't mean to do much talking. (*He comes to* R. *end of the sofa.*)
KIT. But I do. Diana has just this minute given me a message to give you. She wants you to understand that she knows what you feel about her and she's sorry for you. But she must ask you not to take advantage of her pity for you to make her life a burden.
ROGERS. Right. Now that you've had your joke, let me tell you the truth. This afternoon Diana asked me to let you know, in as kindly a way as possible, that her feelings for you have changed entirely, and that she is now in love with me. (*He crosses down* R.)
KIT (*astounded*). God! what nerve! Do you know what she's just said about you? (*Shouting.*) She called you a—silly old bore—

(ROGERS *turns quickly*)

who stuck like a limpet and weren't worth bothering about.

ROGERS. Oh, she did, did she ?

KIT. Yes, she did, and a lot more besides that wouldn't bear repeating.

ROGERS (*taking off his coat and putting it on the armchair down* R.). All right, you lying young fool. I've felt sorry for you up to this, but now I see I've got to teach you a lesson. Put your hands up.

KIT (*putting up his fists*). It's a pleasure. (*He leaps over the sofa to* C.)

(*They stand facing each other, ready for battle. There is a pause. ROGERS suddenly begins to laugh.*)

ROGERS. Good Lord ! (*Collapsing, doubled up with laughter, into the armchair down* R.) You look so damned funny in that get-up.

KIT (*looking down at his legs*). A little eccentric, I admit.

ROGERS. Like a bedraggled old fairy queen.

KIT. I'll go and change. (*He makes for the door up* L.)

ROGERS (*becoming serious*). No, don't. (*Rising.*) If you do I'll have to fight you. I can't when you're looking like that, and if you go on looking like that it'll save us from making idiots of ourselves.

(*They meet* R.C.)

KIT. You know, that's rather sensible. I am surprised.

ROGERS. You know, I'm not quite such a damned fool as you youngsters seem to think. As a matter of fact, I'm a perfectly rational being, and I'm prepared to discuss this particular situation rationally.

KIT. Right. That goes for me too.

(ROGERS *sits on the* R. *edge of the table up* C. KIT *sits at* R. *end of the sofa.*)

ROGERS. Now, I'm ready to admit that you have a grievance against me.

KIT. But I haven't—speaking rationally.

ROGERS. Oh, yes. Rationally speaking, you might say that I've alienated the affections of your sweetheart.

KIT (*smiling*). But you haven't done anything of the sort.

ROGERS (*raising his hand*). Please don't interrupt. Now, I'm perfectly ready to apologize for something that isn't altogether my fault. I hope you will accept it in the spirit in which it is offered.

KIT (*incredulously*). But do you really think Diana's in love with you ?

ROGERS. Certainly.

KIT. Why do you think that ?

ROGERS. She told me so, of course.

KIT (*laughing*). My poor, dear Commander——

ROGERS. I thought we were going to discuss this matter rationally.

KIT. Yes, but when you begin with a flagrant misrepresentation of the facts——

ROGERS. You mean, I'm a liar ? (*He rises.*)

KIT. Yes, that's exactly what I do mean.

ROGERS. Come on. Get up. I see I've got to fight you, skirt or no skirt.

KIT. No, no. Let reason have one last fling. If that fails we can give way to our animal passions. Let me tell you my side of the case.

ROGERS (*sitting again*). All right.

KIT. I've just had a talk with Diana. She said you were in love with her. I suggested to her that it was only fair to you to let you know exactly where you stood—in other words, that she was in love with me and that you had no chance. She answered that, though what I'd said was the truth——

ROGERS. She never said that.

KIT (*raising his hand*). Please don't interrupt. (*Continuing.*) Though what I'd said was the truth, she couldn't tell you because it would be too cruel.

(ROGERS *starts slightly.*)

I then said, rather aptly, that this was a case where she should be cruel only to be kind.

ROGERS. You said what ?

KIT. Cruel only to be kind.

ROGERS. What did she say ?

KIT. She said she found it physically impossible to be cruel. She said she was the sort of person who was miserable if she trod on a snail.

ROGERS. What ! (*He rises and goes towards the window* R.) Are you sure of that ? (*He returns to* C.)

KIT. Certainly.

ROGERS. She said she was miserable if she trod on a snail ?

KIT. Yes.

ROGERS. Good God ! (*He backs to the armchair down* R. *and sits.*)

KIT. What's the matter ?

ROGERS. It's awful ! I can't believe it. I don't believe it. This is all a monstrous plot. (*Swinging round.*) I believe you listened in to my conversation with Diana this afternoon.

KIT. Why ?

ROGERS. Because I also told her she ought to be cruel only to be kind and she made precisely the same answer as she made to you.

KIT (*after a pause*). You mean about the snail ?

ROGERS. Yes, about the snail.

KIT. In other words, she's been double-crossing us. No—you've made all that up.

ROGERS. I only wish I had.

KIT. How do I know you're telling the truth ?

ROGERS. You'll have to take my word for it.
KIT. Why should I ?
ROGERS. Do you want to make me fight you ? (*He rises.*)
KIT (*rising*). Yes, I do. (*He comes up to him.*)

(*There is a pause.*)

ROGERS. Well, I'm not going to. (*He sits in the chair again.*)
KIT. I wonder why it's such a comfort to get away from reason.
ROGERS. Because in this case reason tells us something our vanity won't let us accept.
KIT. It tells us that Diana's a bitch.

(ROGERS *half moves out of his chair.* KIT *sits* R. *on the sofa.*)

Reason. Reason.

(ROGERS *subsides.*)

ROGERS. You're right. We'd better face it. Diana's in love with neither of us and she's made fools out of both of us.
KIT. We don't know that—I mean that she's in love with neither of us. She may be telling lies to one and the truth to the other.
ROGERS. Is that what your reason tells you ?
KIT. No.

(*There is a pause. They are both sunk in gloom.*)

I feel rather sick.
ROGERS. I must have a stronger stomach than you.

(*There is another pause.*)

I suppose you loved her more than I did ?
KIT. Loved her ? I still do love her, damn it.
ROGERS. But you can't, now that you know what you do.
KIT. What difference does that make ? I love her face, I love the way she walks, I love her voice, I love her figure. None of that has changed.
ROGERS (*sympathetically*). Poor boy. It's simpler for me, though it's far more of a shock. You see, what I loved about her was her character.

(*Another pause.*)

KIT. You used to kiss her, I suppose ?
ROGERS (*sadly*). Oh, yes.
KIT. You didn't—you didn't—— ?
ROGERS (*severely*). I loved her for her character. (*After a pause.*)
Did you ?
KIT. Well, no, not really.
ROGERS. I see.

(*Another pause.*)

KIT. What are we going to do ?

(ROGERS *thinks, then rises and comes to* R. *of* KIT.)

ROGERS. We'd better face her together. We'll ask her point-blank which of us she really does love.

KIT. If she says me, I'm done for.￪

ROGERS. But you won't believe her ?

KIT. I'll know she's lying, but I'll believe her all the same.

ROGERS. Well, supposing she says me ?

KIT. That's my only hope.

ROGERS (*patting* KIT *on the shoulder, then moving up* R.). Then, for your sake, I hope she says me.

KIT. That's terribly kind of you, Bill. I say, I may call you Bill, mayn't I ?

ROGERS (*turning*). Oh, my dear Kit.

(*Another pause.*)

You know, what I feel like doing is to go out and get very drunk.

KIT. Suppose we go and throw ourselves into the sea instead of going to the Casino.

ROGERS. I think my idea is better.

KIT. Yes, perhaps you're right. (*Rising.*) Then let's start now.

ROGERS. You can't go out like that, my dear Kit.

KIT. Then let's go to the Casino.

ROGERS. I haven't got anything to wear.

KIT (*holding out the tunic*). Wear this over your flannels.

ROGERS. All right. Help me put it on.

(ALAN *and* BRIAN *come in up* R.   KIT *is buttoning up* ROGERS' *tunic. They both stop in amazement.*)

ALAN. What on earth——?

KIT (*excitedly*). Bill and I are going to the Casino, Alan. You've got to come too.

ALAN. Bill and you. What is this ? Some new sort of game ?

KIT. Go and put something on. You come too, Brian.

BRIAN (*coming down* R.). No, old boy. Not me.

KIT (*moving up* R.). Go on, Alan. We want to get out of the house before Diana arrives. Where is she, by the way ?

ROGERS (R.C.). Who cares !

(KIT *laughs.*)

ALAN (*between* KIT *and* ROGERS—*scratching his head*). Let me get this straight. You want me to come to the Ball with you and the Commander——

KIT. Don't call him the Commander, Alan. His name is Bill.

ALAN. Bill ?

KIT. Yes, Bill. He's one of the best fellows in the world.

ROGERS. We're going to get drunk together, aren't we, Kit ?

ALAN.   Kit ?

KIT.   Screaming drunk, Bill.

ALAN (*dashing to the door up* L.).   I won't be a minute.

(*He goes up* L.)

BRIAN.   This sounds like a party.

KIT.   Brian, tell me how I can get hold of your Chi-Chi.   Is she going to the Casino to-night ?

BRIAN.   Yes, old boy.

KIT.   How can I recognize her ?

BRIAN.   I don't think you can miss her.   She's not likely to miss you, anyway, if you go into the bar alone.

KIT.   Has she got a good figure ?

BRIAN.   I like it, but I'm easy to please.   From sideways on it's a bit S-shaped, if you know what I mean.

(ALAN *re-enters with his German coat and crosses to the window up* R.)

ALAN.   I shall probably be lynched in this thing.   ˙

KIT.   Come on.   Let's go.

(ROGERS *goes to the window,* KIT *following.   They stand on the step while* ALAN *is putting on his German coat.   The three are about to go off when* BRIAN *calls them back.*)

BRIAN.   Hi !   Wait a minute.   What am I to tell Diana ?

(*They stop.*)

ROGERS.   Tell her we're being cruel only to be kind.

KIT.   Tell her to be careful she doesn't go treading on any snails.

ALAN.   Just tell her to go to hell.   That leaves no room for doubt.

(*They go out.* BRIAN *stands gazing after them.*)

CURTAIN.

ACT III

SCENE 1

SCENE.—*The same.*

TIME.—*A few hours later.*

The CURTAIN *rises to disclose* ALAN *lying on the sofa* L.C. *and* KIT *sitting in the armchair down* R. *hugging the cushion—both smoking cigars.* ROGERS *is on the floor at* R. *end of the sofa, leaning against it with a cushion for his head. He does not smoke ; he is in a sleepy mood and slightly drunk. They are in the same clothes in which they had gone to the Casino.*

KIT (*drowsily*). I don't agree with you. I don't agree with you at all. You can't judge women by our standards of Right and Wrong.

ALAN. They have none of their own, so how can you judge them ?

KIT. Why judge them at all ? There they are—all of them, I grant you, behaving absolutely nohow—still that's what they're for, I mean they're built that way, and you've just got to take them or leave them. I'll take them.

ROGERS (*murmuring dreamily*). I'll take vanilla.

KIT. Now, you tell me that Diana's a trollop. All right. I shan't deny it. I shall only say that I, personally, like trollops.

ALAN. But you can like them without loving them. I mean, love is only sublimated sex, isn't it ?

ROGERS (*rousing himself a little*). Devilish funny thing—my old friend Freud, the last time I met him, said *exactly* the same thing. Bill, old man, he said, take my word for it, love is only sublimated sex. (*Composing himself for sleep again.*) That's what dear Old Freudie said.

ALAN. I fear that Bill is what he'd describe himself as half-seas over.

KIT. He's lucky. The more I drank up at that foul Casino, the more sober I became. What were you saying about sublimated sex ?

ALAN. Only that if that's what you feel for Diana, why sublimate ?

(ROGERS *has gradually been sinking on to the floor. He is now stretched out on the floor.*)

54

KIT.   Ah! Because she's clever enough to give me no choice.

ALAN.   How simple everything would be if that sort of so-called virtue were made illegal—if it were just a question of will you or won't you.   No one ought to be allowed to get away with that—I'd like to, but I mustn't.   It's that that leads to all the trouble. The Commander has now definitely passed out.   You know, I like him, Kit.   It's quite amazing how pleasant he is when you get to know him.

KIT.   Yes, I know.

ALAN.   Do you realize that if it hadn't been for Diana, we'd probably have gone on disliking him for ever ?

KIT.   Yes.   We've got to be grateful to her for that.

ALAN.   I wonder *why* we disliked him so much before to-night ?

ROGERS (*turning on his back*).   I'll tell you.

ALAN.   Good Lord!   I thought you'd passed out.

ROGERS.   Officers in the Royal Navy never pass out.

ALAN.   They just fall on the floor in an alcoholic stupor, I suppose ?

ROGERS.   Exactly.

KIT.   Well, tell us why we disliked you so much.

ROGERS (*struggling to sit up*).   Right.

(ALAN *helps him up and then places the cushion behind his head.*)

Thank you, my dear fellow.   Because you all made up your mind to dislike me before I ever came into the house.   All except Diana, that's to say.   From the moment I arrived, you all treated me as if I were some interesting old relic of a bygone age.   I've never known such an unfriendly lot of blighters as you all were.

ALAN.   We thought you were a bumptious bore.

ROGERS (*turning slowly and looking at* ALAN).   Oh, I may have seemed a bortious bump, but that was only because I was in a blue funk of you all.   Here was I, who'd never been away from my ship for more than a few days at a time, suddenly plumped down in a house full of strange people, all talking either French, which I couldn't understand, or your own brand of English, which was almost as hard, and all convinced I was a half-wit.   Of course I was in a blue funk.

ALAN.   Well, I'm damned.

ROGERS.   As a matter of fact, I liked you all.

ALAN.   Oh, that's very gratifying.

ROGERS.   I didn't agree with most of your opinions, but I enjoyed listening to them.   I wanted to discuss them with you, but I was never given the chance.   You all seemed to think that because I was in the Navy I was incapable of consecutive thought—I say, whisky doesn't half loosen the old tongue.

ALAN.   But you always seemed so aggressive.

ROGERS.   I was only defending myself.   You attacked first, you know.

ALAN (*contritely*).   I'm terribly sorry.

ROGERS.   That's all right.   As a matter of fact, it's done me a lot of good being here.   One gets into a bit of a rut, you know, in the Service.   One's apt to forget that there are some people in the world who have different ideas and opinions to one's own. You'll find the same in the Diplomatic.

ALAN.   I know.   That's one of the reasons I want to chuck it.

(ROGERS *rises gingerly on to the end of the sofa, looking into* ALAN's *face.   ALAN thinks he might kiss him, so gradually slips down the sofa farther away, looks surprised and takes a deep puff at his cigar.*)

ROGERS.   Will you let me give you a bit of advice about that ? I've been wanting to for a long time, but I've always been afraid you'd bite my head off if I did.

ALAN.   Of course.

ROGERS.   Well, chuck it.   Go and do your writing.

ALAN (*sitting up*).   I'd go back to England to-morrow, only——
(*He stops.*)

ROGERS.   Only what ?

ALAN.   I don't know if I can write, for one thing.

ROGERS.   It's ten to one you can't, but I shouldn't let that stop you.   If it's what you want to do, I should do it.

ALAN.   That isn't the real reason.

ROGERS.   You haven't got the guts, is that it ?

ALAN.   That isn't quite my way of putting it, but I suppose it's true.   I can't bring myself to make a definite decision.   I'm afraid of my father, of course.   But it's not only that.   (*He puts his cigar out in the ashtray beside him, rises and takes the ashtray to the table* L. *He leaves it there, then returns and sits on the sofa again.*) I admit that there are a dozen things I'd rather do than the Diplomatic.   It's an exciting world at the moment.   Do you know, sometimes I think I'll go and fight.   There must be a war on somewhere.

ROGERS.   I thought you were a pacifist.

ALAN.   Oh, what the hell ?—I shall become a diplomat.

ROGERS.   You'll be a damned bad one.

ALAN.   I can adapt myself.

ROGERS (*rising, yawning—hugging the cushion he had for his head*). Well, I've given you my advice for what it's worth.   I shall now go to bed to sleep the sleep of the very drunk.

ALAN.   You mustn't go yet.   You've got to wait for Diana.

ROGERS (*with a magnificent gesture*).   Diana—pooh !

ALAN.   It's all very well for you to say, " Diana—pooh ! " but this weak-kneed, jelly-livered protoplasm here is still in her clutches.

KIT (*who has been musing*).   Are you referring to me ?

ALAN.   Diana's only got to raise her little finger and he'll go rushing back to her, screaming to be forgiven.

ROGERS (*backing up* C.). Then we must stop her raising her little finger.

ALAN. Exactly. That's why we must face her together.

ROGERS (*sitting down with a bump on the table-bench*). The United Front. We must scupper her with a plunging salvo.

ALAN. Oh, no, don't let's do that.

KIT (*dismally*). She's only got to say she still loves me.

ALAN. My dear Kit, if she has to choose between you and Bill, she'll choose you. You're younger, you're better-looking, and you've got more money. Don't you agree, Bill ?

ROGERS. He's certainly younger and he's certainly got more money.

ALAN (*to* KIT). You must be firm, you must be strong. If you show any weakness, you'll be a traitor to our sex.

ROGERS. By Jove, yes. We must put up a good show in this engagement.

KIT. It's all very well for you to talk. You don't know——

ALAN. Haven't I resisted her attacks for a whole month ?

KIT. They were only little skirmishes. You don't know what it is to receive the whole brunt of her attack. It's quite hopeless. You can help me as much as you like, but if she attacks me directly, I shall go under, I know that.

ALAN. Do you hear that, Commander ? I submit that he be tried for Extreme Cowardice in the face of the Enemy. (*He sits upon the sofa.*)

ROGERS (*throwing his cushion down on the table up* C.). The Court finds the prisoner guilty. (*Rising with dignity.*) Mr. Neilan, I must call upon you to surrender your trousers. Ah ! I see you have come into court without them. Very well, I have no option but to ask you for your skirt.

KIT. Come and get it.

ROGERS (*moving down to* KIT). I've been longing to get my hands on that damn thing all the evening. Come on, Alan.

(KIT *leaps out of his chair, and runs across the room, pursued by* ROGERS. *He is cornered by* ALAN *and there is a scuffle. Eventually they all land on the floor in front of the sofa :* ROGERS R., ALAN C., KIT L.

DIANA, *stately and sad, comes through the French windows. She stands in the doorway for some five seconds before* ROGERS *sees her.*)

Crikey !

(*He taps the other two on the shoulders and they straighten themselves. There is a rather nervous silence.*)

DIANA (*coming into the room*). Well—I hope you all enjoyed yourselves at the Casino.

ROGERS (*after glancing àt the others*). Oh, yes. Thanks very much.

DIANA.   Brian gave me a message from you which I found rather hard to understand.   Perhaps you'd explain it now.

(*There is a pause.*   ALAN *looks inquiringly from* KIT *to* ROGERS. ROGERS *looks appealingly at* ALAN.)

ALAN.   Well, who is to fire the first shot of the salvo ?

(*There is no answer.*)

Come, come, gentlemen.

(*Still no answer.*)

Very well, I must engage the enemy on your behalf.   Diana, these two gentlemen have good reason to believe that you have been trifling with their affections.   You have told Kit that you are in love with him and are bored by Bill, and you have told Bill that you are in love with him and are bored by Kit.   So now they naturally want to know who exactly you are in love with and who exactly you are bored by.

ROGERS (*nodding vigorously*).   Yes, that's right.

DIANA (*with scorn*).   Oh, do they ?

ALAN.   Are you going to answer their question ?

DIANA.   Certainly not.   Whom I love and whom I don't love is entirely my own affair.   I've never heard such insolence.

ALAN (*turning to* ROGERS *and* KIT—*chuckling*).   Insolence ! She's good, this girl, she's very good.

(DIANA *attempts to go, but* ALAN *jumps up and catches her by the wrist.*)

DIANA (*patiently*).   May I please be allowed to go to my room ?

ALAN (*barring her way*).   Not until you've answered our question.

DIANA.   I think you'd better let me go.

ALAN.   Just as soon as you've given a straight answer to a straight question.

DIANA (*shaking her hand loose from* ALAN).   All right.   You want to know who I'm in love with.   Well, I'll tell you.   (*To* ALAN.) I'm in love with you.

(ALAN *recoils.   There is a dead silence.*)

Good night !

(*She exits up* L.   ROGERS *and* KIT *turn on the floor to watch her go. Then* ROGERS *rises and backs up* R.C.   ALAN *falls limply into the armchair down* R.)

ROGERS (*scratching his head*).   Now, will someone tell me, was our engagement a success ?

ALAN (*bitterly*).   A success ?   (*Groaning.*)   Oh, what a girl, what a girl !

(ROGERS *comes down to* R. *of* ALAN.)

KIT (*gloomily*). It was a success as far as I'm concerned.

(*There is a pause.* KIT *rises to* C.)

ALAN.　I'm frightened. I'm really frightened.

ROGERS.　What ? (*Sternly, putting a hand on* ALAN'S *shoulder.*) Alan, I never thought to hear such words from you.

ALAN.　I can't help it. I shall fall. Oh, God! I know it, I shall fall.

ROGERS.　You must be firm. You must be strong. The United Front must not be broken.

ALAN.　I want you to promise me something, you two. You must never, never leave me alone with that girl.

ROGERS.　That sounds like rank cowardice.

ALAN.　Cowardice be damned! You don't realize the appalling danger I'm in. If I'm left alone with her for a minute, I shudder to think what might happen. She might even (*in a whisper*) marry me.

ROGERS.　Oh, not that.

ALAN.　It's true. God help me. I think she may easily try to marry me. (*Turning imploringly to the others.*) So you see, you can't desert me now. Don't let me out of your sight for a second. Even if I beg you on my knees to leave me alone with her, don't do it. Will you promise ?

ROGERS.　I promise.

ALAN.　And you, Kit ?

(KIT *nods. They each shake hands with* ALAN *in turn.*)

Thank you. (*He rises to up* C.) I've only got three weeks before the exam., but that's a long time with Diana in the house.

ROGERS (*crossing to* R. *of* ALAN). I think your hope lies in this Lord Heybrook fellow who's coming to-morrow.

(KIT *moves down* L.)

She may easily find that a peer in hand is worth more than one in the vague future. I shall go to bed. (*He crosses* ALAN *to the door up* L.) Good night, Alan. You have my best wishes. (*At the door.*) Don't go down to breakfast to-morrow until I come and fetch you. Good night, Kit.

(*He goes out.*)

ALAN.　There's a real friend. I hope you're going to show the same self-sacrifice.

KIT.　I don't know what you're making all the fuss about. You ought to be very happy.

ALAN.　Happy ? (*Sarcastically.*) I've noticed how happy you've been these last few weeks.

KIT　I have in a way. (*He sits at* R. *end of the sofa.*)

ALAN.　That's not my way. Damn it, Kit, I'm a man with

principles and ideals. I'm a romantic. Let me give you a little word-picture of the girl I should like to fall in love with. Then you can tell how far it resembles Diana. First of all, she must not be a trollop.

KIT (*shrugging indifferently*). Oh, well, of course——

ALAN (*walking up and down from the window to* R. *end of the sofa*). Secondly, she will be able to converse freely and intelligently with me on all subjects—Politics—Philosophy—Religion—— Thirdly, she will have all the masculine virtues and none of the feminine vices. Fourthly, she will be physically unattractive enough to keep her faithful to me, and attractive enough to make me desire her. Fifthly, she will be in love with me. That's all, I think.

KIT. You don't want much, do you? I admit it isn't a close description of Diana, but where on earth do you expect to find this love-dream?

ALAN. They do exist, you know. There's someone here, in this house, who answers to all the qualifications, except the last.

KIT (*sitting forward*). Good Lord! You don't mean Jack, do you?

ALAN. Why not?

KIT. But—but you couldn't be in love with Jack.

ALAN. I'm not, but she's exactly the sort of girl I should like to be in love with.

KIT (*smiling*). Love and Jack. They just don't seem to connect. I'm frightfully fond of her, but somehow—I don't know—I mean you couldn't kiss her or make love to her.

ALAN. Why not try it and see?

KIT. Who? Me? Good Lord, no.

ALAN. Don't you think she's attractive?

KIT. Yes, I suppose she is, in a way, very attractive. But don't you see, Alan, I know her far too well to start any hanky-panky. She'd just scream with laughter.

ALAN. Really? (*He crosses to the armchair down* R., *sits and lights a cigarette from the box on the table beside him.*) She'd just scream with laughter? (*Turning on him.*) You poor idiot, don't you realize the girl's been madly in love with you for two months now?

KIT (*after a pause, derisively*). Ha, ha!

ALAN. All right. Say ha, ha. Don't believe it, and forget I ever said it. I promised her I'd never tell you.

(*There is a pause.* KIT *rises and goes to* ALAN.)

KIT. What did you have to drink up at the Casino?

ALAN. Less than you.

KIT. Are you stone-cold sober?

ALAN. As sober as ten Lady Astors.

KIT. And you sit there and tell me——

(*Voices are heard outside.* KIT *tries to escape through the door up* L., *but is too late.* MAINGOT *comes in, followed by* JACQUELINE.)

MAINGOT. Aha! Le Grec et l'Allemand. Vous vous êtes bien amusés au Casino ?

JACQUELINE. Hello, Kit.

ALAN. Très bien, monsieur. Et vous ?

(MAINGOT *sits at* R. *end of the table-bench and changes his slippers.* JACQUELINE *crosses and sits at* R. *end of the sofa.* KIT *stands gaping open-mouthed at her.*)

MAINGOT. Ah, oui! C'était assez gai, mais on y a mangé excessivement mal, et le champagne était très mauvais et m'a coûté les yeux de la tête. Quand même le quatorze ne vient qu'une fois par an. (*Rising.*) Alors, je vais me coucher. Bonsoir, bonne nuit et dormez bien.

ALL. Bonsoir, bonne nuit.

(MAINGOT *goes out up* L. *with his shoes.*)

JACQUELINE. Why did you all leave so early ?

KIT (*gaping*). Oh, I don't know.

JACQUELINE. Your costume caused a sensation, Kit. Everyone was asking me what it was meant to be.

(KENNETH *enters up* R. *and comes to* C.)

KIT (*nervously*). Really.

ALAN. Did you have a good time, Kenneth ?

KENNETH. Oh, all right. I'll say good night. I've got an essay to finish before to-morrow.

JACQUELINE. Good night, Kenneth, and thank you.

KENNETH. Good night.

(*He goes out up* L., *looking very sulky.*)

ALAN. You must have had a wonderful time with the Babe in that mood.

JACQUELINE (*putting her hat on the sofa*). What's the matter with him, Alan ?

ALAN. He's angry with me for not doing his essay for him. (*Rising and crossing to the door up* L.) I think I'd better go and make my peace with him. (*At the door.*) Don't go to bed for a few minutes. I want to talk to you, Jack.

(*He goes out. There is a pause.* KIT *is plainly uncomfortable.*)

KIT (*at* L. *end of the sofa*). Jack.

JACQUELINE. Yes ?

KIT. Did you have a good time to-night ?

JACQUELINE (*puzzled*). Yes, thank you, Kit.

KIT. Good. (*He moves slowly round back of the sofa to* R. *of her.*) I—er—I'm sorry I couldn't take you.

JACQUELINE. That's all right. (*Smiling.*) That was Brian's girl you and Alan were dancing with, wasn't it ? What's she like ?

KIT. Pretty hellish.

(*There is a pause.*)

Jack.

JACQUELINE. Yes ?

KIT. Oh, nothing. (*He wanders forlornly about the room.*) **Was** it raining when you came back ?

JACQUELINE. No, it wasn't raining.

KIT. It was when we came back.

JACQUELINE. Really ?

(*There is a pause.*)

KIT. Yes, quite heavily.

JACQUELINE. It must have cleared up, then.

(KIT *takes out a cigarette-case from his hip-pocket.*)

KIT (*turning with sudden decision*). Jack, there's something I must—— (*In turning he opens his case and spills all the cigarettes on the floor.*)

JACQUELINE (*rising and kneeling on the floor with* KIT *to pick up the cigarettes*). I've never seen a clumsier idiot than you, Kit. I seem to spend my life cleaning up after you. (*She puts the cigarettes in the case and hands it back to him.*) There !

(KIT *kisses her suddenly and clumsily on the mouth. She pushes him away. They are both embarrassed and puzzled.*)

You smell of whisky, Kit.

(ALAN *enters up* L. *and comes to* L.C.)

ALAN. Oh !

KIT (*rising*). I'm going to bed. Good night.

(*He goes out up* L.)

JACQUELINE. What's the matter with him ? Is he drunk ?

ALAN. No, Jack, but I've a confession to make to you.

JACQUELINE (*in alarm*). You haven't told him ?

ALAN (*sitting on the sofa*). I couldn't help it.

JACQUELINE (*rising*). Oh, Alan, no.

ALAN. Will you forgive me ?

JACQUELINE. I'll never forgive you. It's ruined everything. (*A shade tearfully.*) He's just been talking to me about the weather.

ALAN. Well, he's a bit embarrassed, naturally.

JACQUELINE (*walking up to the window, then back round behind the sofa to up* C.). But he'll spend all his time running away from me now, and when he is with me he'll always be wondering if I want him to kiss me, and he'll go on talking about the weather, and—(*turning away*)—oh, it's awful !

ALAN. I'm sorry, Jack. I meant well. (*He rises and goes up to* L. *of her.*)

JACQUELINE. Men are such blundering fools.

ALAN. Yes, I suppose we are. Will you forgive me?

JACQUELINE (*wearily*). Of course I forgive you. (*She goes below the sofa, picks up her hat, then passes round* L. *of the sofa to the door up* L.) I'm going to bed.

ALAN. All right. We'll talk about it in the morning. I may be able to persuade Kit I was joking.

JACQUELINE (*at the door*). No. Please don't say anything more to Kit. You've done enough harm as it is. (*Relenting.*) Good night, Alan. You're just a sentimental old monster, aren't you?

ALAN. Who, me?

JACQUELINE. Yes, you. Good night.

(*She goes out.* ALAN *stands alone for a moment, then goes to door up* L. *and opens it.*)

ALAN (*calling*). Jack.

JACQUELINE (*off*). Yes?

ALAN. Will you see if Brian's in his room. I want to lock up.

JACQUELINE (*off*). Right. (*After a pause.*) No, he must still be out.

ALAN. I'll leave a note for him.

(*He closes the door, then crosses to the table* R.C., *puts out his cigarette and starts to write a note on a scribbling-block on the table. While he is writing* DIANA *comes in softly and stands behind him. He doesn't hear her.*)

DIANA (*gently*). Alan.

ALAN (*jumping up*). Oh, God!

DIANA. Do you mind if I speak to you for a moment?

ALAN. Well, I was just going to bed.

(*He attempts to escape through the window up* R., *but she catches his arm.*)

DIANA (*inexorably*). I suppose you didn't believe what I told you just now.

ALAN (*looking despairingly round for help*). No, I didn't believe it.

DIANA (*with quiet resignation*). No—I knew you wouldn't, and, of course, after what's happened I couldn't expect you to. But, whether you believe me or not, I just want to say this.

ALAN (*wildly, crossing in front of* DIANA *and trying to escape the other way*). In the morning, Diana—say it in the morning. I'm frightfully tired and——

DIANA (*catching him at* R. *end of the sofa*). Please listen to me.

(ALAN *groans and sits on the* R. *arm of the sofa.*)

I just wanted to say that it's been you from the first moment we met. Kit and Bill never meant a thing to me. I let them think

I was in love with them. But it was only because I had some idea it might make you jealous.

ALAN. It's a pity you didn't succeed.

DIANA (*breaking away to* R.). Oh, I know what you think of me, and you're quite right, I suppose. (*Pathetically.*) I've told so many lies before that I can't expect you to believe me when I'm telling the truth.

ALAN. Poor little Matilda.

DIANA. But this is the truth, now. (*Going up to him and playing with his shirt-collar.*) This is the only completely sincere feeling I've ever had for anyone in all my life. (*Simply.*) I *do* love you, Alan. I always have and suppose I always will.

ALAN (*in agony*). Oh, go away. Please go away.

DIANA. All right. (*Going up* L.) I know you have every right to think I'm lying, but I'm not, Alan, really, I'm not; that's what's so funny.

ALAN (*imploringly*). Oh, God help me!

DIANA (*at the door*). Good night, Alan. (*Simply.*) I do love you.

ALAN (*rising*). Say that again, blast you!

DIANA. I love you.

(*He goes to meet her up* L. *and embraces her fervently.*)

(*Emerging from the embrace—ecstatically.*) I suppose this is true.

ALAN. You know damn well it is.

DIANA. Say it, darling.

ALAN (*hedging*). Say what?

DIANA. Say you love me.

ALAN. Must I? (*Crossing up* C.) Oh, this is hell! (*Shouting.*) I love you.

DIANA (*turning back rapturously*). Alan, darling——

(BRIAN *comes in through the window.*)

BRIAN. Hullo, Alan. Hullo, Diana, old thing.

(DIANA *looks through* BRIAN *and turns hurriedly to the door.*)

DIANA (*softly*). Good night, Alan. I'll see you in the morning.

(*She goes out up* L.)

BRIAN. Did you see that, old boy? She cut me dead. She's furious with me. (*He sits on the* L. *arm of the chair down* R.) I must tell you about it, because it's a damned funny story. After you boys had gone I took Diana to have a bite of dinner with me. Well, we had a bottle of wine and got pretty gay, and all the time she was giving me the old green light.

ALAN. The green light? (*He remains* C.)

BRIAN. Yes. The go-ahead signal. Well, after a bit I rather handed out an invitation to the waltz, if you follow me.

ALAN. Yes. I follow you.

BRIAN.   I mean, everybody being out, it seemed an opportunity not to be missed.   Well, do you know what she did then, old boy ?
ALAN.   No.
BRIAN.   She gave me a sharp buffet on the kisser.
ALAN.   What did you do ?
BRIAN.   I said, well, if that isn't what you want, what the hell do you want ?   Then she got up and left me.   I never laughed so much in my life.
ALAN (*dazedly*).   You laughed ?
BRIAN.   Wouldn't you, old boy ?

(ALAN *gazes at him with amazed admiration.*)

Well, I'm for bed.   (*He rises and crosses to* L.)   I say, I met the most charming little girl just now on the front—fantastic piece she was.   She gave me her card.   (*He sits at* L. *end of the sofa.*)   Yes, here it is.   Colette, chez Madame Pontet, Rue Lafayette Twenty-three.   Bains fifty francs.   I think I shall pop round to-morrow and have a bain.
ALAN (*sitting at* R. *end of the sofa and gazing at* BRIAN *with awe*).
Oh, Brian !   How right-minded you are !
BRIAN.   Me ?
ALAN.   Thank God you came in when you did.   You don't know what you've done for me with your splendid shining example.   I now see my way clear before me.   A great light has dawned.
BRIAN.   I say, old boy, are you feeling all right ?
ALAN.   Listen, Brian.   You weren't the only person to get the old green light from Diana to-night.   I got it too.
BRIAN.   Doesn't surprise me.   I should think she's pretty stingy with her yellows and reds.
ALAN.   Yes, but I didn't respond to it in the same glorious way as you.   However, what's done can be undone.   (*Rising and going to the door up* L.)   I am now going upstairs to put the same question to Diana as you did earlier in the evening.
BRIAN.   I shouldn't, old boy.   She'll say no, and believe me, she's got rather a painful way of saying it.
ALAN.   If she says no, then, lacking your own sterling qualities, I shan't pay a visit to Rue Lafayette Twenty-three.   No.   I shall run away.   I shall go back to London to-morrow.
BRIAN.   But what about your exam. and so forth ?
ALAN.   I shall chuck that.   (*Opening the door.*)   I am now about to throw my future life into the balance of fate.   Diplomat or writer.   Which shall it be ?   Diana shall choose.

(*He exits up* L.)

BRIAN.   I don't know what he's talking about.   He's crackers !

(BRIAN *shakes his head wonderingly.   After a bit he rises and crosses to the table* R.C., *where he stops to think.*)

Bains fifty francs! (*He fumbles for money and starts to count.*)
Twenty—thirty—forty—forty-three—Damn!

(*A door-slam is heard off* L. ALAN *returns and puts his head through
the door up* L.)

ALAN. I'm going to be a writer. Come and help me pack.

(*His head disappears.* BRIAN *crosses and follows him out, murmuring
expostulations.*)

CURTAIN.

SCENE 2

SCENE.—*The same.*

TIME.—*The next morning. After breakfast.*

When the CURTAIN *rises* MARIANNE *exits down* L. *with a tray.* JAC-
QUELINE *is folding up the tablecloth* L.C. KENNETH *comes in from
the window,* MAINGOT *following. They have evidently just finished
a lesson.*

MAINGOT (*at the window*). Il ne vaut pas la peine de continuer.
Vous n'en saurez jamais rien. Dites à Monsieur Curtis que je l'attends.
KENNETH. Oui, monsieur.
MAINGOT. Je serai dans le jardin. Oh, ma petite Jacqueline
que j'ai mal à la tête ce matin.
JACQUELINE. Pauvre papa. Je suis bien fâchée.
MAINGOT. Ça passera—ça passera. Heureusement le quatorze
ne vient qu'une fois par an.
KENNETH (*at the door up* L., *calling*). Brian!
BRIAN (*off*). Yes, old boy?

(MAINGOT *exits up* R.)

KENNETH. Your lesson.
BRIAN (*off*). Won't be a second.

(KENNETH *closes the door and wanders mournfully over to the bookcase
and puts his books away.*)

JACQUELINE. Why so sad this morning, Kenneth?
KENNETH. You've heard the news about Alan?
JACQUELINE. Yes, my father told me.
KENNETH. Don't you think it's awful?
JACQUELINE. No. For one thing, I don't believe for a moment
he's serious.
KENNETH. Oh, he's serious all right. What a damn fool!
If I had half his chance of getting in the Diplomatic I wouldn't go
and chuck it up.

(BRIAN *comes in up* L., *carrying a sheet of paper and a notebook.*)

BRIAN. 'Morning, all. Where's Maingot père?

(JACQUELINE *takes off her overall and comes down* L.)

KENNETH. He's waiting for you in the garden.

BRIAN. Oh! (*Anxiously.*) Tell me, old boy, how is he this morning? Gay, happy—at peace with the world?

KENNETH. No. He's got a bad headache, and he's in a fiendish temper.

(*He goes out up* L.)

BRIAN. Couple of portos too many last night, I fear.

JACQUELINE. Why this tender anxiety for my father's health, Brian?

(JACQUELINE *puts her overall on chair* 5, *where the tablecloth also is.*)

BRIAN (*above chair* 4). Well, Jack, I'm afraid I may have to deliver a rather rude shock to his nervous system. You see, I'm supposed to have done an essay on the Waterloo campaign, and what with one thing and another I don't seem to have got awfully far.

JACQUELINE. How far?

BRIAN (*reading*). La bataille de Waterloo était gagnée sur les champs d'Eton.

JACQUELINE. And that's the essay, is it?

(BRIAN *nods.*)

Well, if I were you, I shouldn't show it to him. I'd tell him you did one of five pages and it got lost.

BRIAN (*doubtfully*). Yes. But something seems to tell me he won't altogether credit that story.

(MAINGOT *comes in up* R. JACQUELINE *exits down* L. *with her overall and tablecloth.*)

MAINGOT. Eh bien, Monsieur Curtis, qu'est-ce qu'on attend? Vous êtes en retard.

BRIAN. Ah, monsieur, vous êtes bon—ce matin, j'espère?

MAINGOT. Non, j'ai affreusement mal à la tête.

BRIAN (*sympathetically*). Oh! C'est trop mauvais. A trifle hung-over, peutêtre? Un tout petit peu suspendu.

MAINGOT. Vous êtes fou ce matin?

BRIAN (*following* MAINGOT *off up* R.). Il est très dommage—— J'ai perdu mon essai.

(*They disappear.* MAINGOT *is heard expostulating.* JACQUELINE *re-enters and runs across to the window up* R. *The door up* L. *opens very slowly and* ALAN'S *head appears.*)

ALAN (*whispering*). Jack!

JACQUELINE (*turning*). Hallo, Alan.

ALAN. Is Diana about?

JACQUELINE. She's in the garden. She wants to speak to you.

ALAN. I bet she does. But I'm taking good care she doesn't get a chance.

(*He comes cautiously into the room. He is dressed in a lounge suit preparatory for going away.*)

I want to get my books together. (*He goes to the bookcase.*)

JACQUELINE. Alan, you're not serious about this, are you?

ALAN. Never more serious in my life, Jack. (*He is collecting books from the bookcase.*)

JACQUELINE. You're breaking Diana's heart, you know.

ALAN. Ha! Is that what she told you?

JACQUELINE. Oh, no. She wouldn't give herself away to me, but I honestly think she is rather in love with you, Alan.

ALAN. Yes, that's just what I'm afraid of.

JACQUELINE. You know, you're the only man in the world who's ever got away from Diana unscathed.

ALAN (*turning quickly*). Don't say that! It's unlucky. I'm not out of the house yet.

(*He turns back to the bookcase as DIANA comes running into the room from the garden.*)

JACQUELINE (*quickly*). Look out, Alan.

ALAN (*seeing DIANA*). Oh, my God!

(*He darts out of the room, dropping all his books as he does so. DIANA kicks at the books, then walks backwards and forwards behind the table.*)

DIANA. It's no good. He's sure to have locked the door of his room. I'm afraid he's quite determined to go. I feel dreadfully bad about it, because I'm responsible for the whole thing. All this talk of writing is just nonsense. He's only running away from me.

JACQUELINE (*sitting in the armchair down* R.). I don't altogether blame him.

DIANA. I suppose it's a wonderful compliment for a man to throw up his career just for my sake, but I can't see it that way. I'm really frightfully upset.

JACQUELINE. You don't look it.

DIANA. But I am; honestly I am. You see, I can't understand why he should want to run away from me. I can't see what he's got to be frightened of.

JACQUELINE. Can't you?

DIANA (*going to the door up* L. *and looking out*). If only I could get a chance to talk to him alone, I'm sure I could persuade him not to go.

JACQUELINE. I'm sure you could, too. So is Alan. But I don't think you'll get the chance.

(MARIANNE *comes in from the kitchen*.)

MARIANNE (*to* JACQUELINE). S'il vous plaît, mam'selle, voulez vous monter voir la chambre de Lord Heybrook. Je l'ai preparée.

JACQUELINE. Bien, Marianne. (*She rises.*) Je viens tout de suite.

(MARIANNE *goes out, and* JACQUELINE *follows her to the door.*)

DIANA (*up* C.). Oh, does this Lord Heybrook arrive this morning ?

JACQUELINE. Yes. That's a thought to console you, isn't it ?

(*She exits down* L. DIANA *goes to the window up* R. *and looks out. The door up* L. *opens and* ROGERS *and* ALAN *look through.* ALAN *signs to* ROGERS *to go first, which he does,* ALAN *following.* ROGERS *attempts to pick up the books, but makes a noise in doing so, and* DIANA *hears him and turns round.* ROGERS *takes a position,* C., *between* ALAN *and* DIANA, *nonchalantly looking up at the ceiling.*)

DIANA (*quietly*). Do you mind going away, please, Bill ? I want to talk to Alan alone.

ROGERS (*paying no attention*). Well, it's . . .

DIANA (*shortly*). Bill, did you hear me ? I asked you to go.

ROGERS. I'm sorry, I can't.

DIANA (*realizing the situation and stepping back with dignity*). Do you think it's necessary to behave like this ?

ALAN. You can say anything you want to say in front of Bill.

(ROGERS *and* ALAN *smile at each other.*)

DIANA. No, thank you. I'd rather not.

ALAN. Then you don't say it.

DIANA (*above chair* 1—*after a slight pause*). All right, if you're determined to be so childish. This is all I want to say. (*With great sincerity.*) Alan, you know your own mind. If you feel you must run away from me, go ahead. I won't try to stop you. I only hope you'll be happy without me. I know I shan't be happy without you.

ALAN (*who in spite of the rock-like presence of* ROGERS *is beginning to fall*). You'll get over it.

(*He crosses to* R. *of* ROGERS, *who pulls him back by the arm. They bow to each other.*)

DIANA. Oh, I expect so. You'll write to me occasionally, won't you ?

ALAN. Oh, yes, every day, if you like.

DIANA (*going to* ALAN). I'd like to know how you're getting on in your new career. I wish you the very, very best of luck.

ALAN. Thank you.

DIANA. I'll be thinking of you a lot.

ALAN (*weakening again, going up to* DIANA). It's very kind of you to say so.

DIANA. Well, that's really all I wanted to say, only . . . (*falteringly*) I would rather like to say good-bye, and that's a bit hard with Bill standing there like the Rock of Gibraltar.

(*There is a long pause while* ALAN *wrestles with himself.*)

ALAN (*suddenly*). Bill, get out.

(ROGERS *doesn't budge.*)

Get out, Bill.

(ROGERS *seems not to have heard.* ALAN *approaches him menacingly.*)

Get out, blast you!

ROGERS (*slowly*). Is that the voice of reason, my dear fellow?

(ALAN *stares at him and suddenly collects himself.*)

ALAN. Oh, thank you, Bill.

(*They both pick up the remaining books and exit up* L.)

DIANA. Here, you've forgotten some. (*She throws the books after them, then goes to the door down* L. *and calls.*) Marianne. A quelle heure arrive ce Lord Heybrook?

JACQUELINE (*calling from the kitchen*). Lord Heybrook's arriving at ten-fifteen. (*She appears in the doorway.*) He'll be here any moment now.

DIANA (*annoyed*). Oh, thank you very much. (*She goes to* R. *end of the table-bench and sits.*)

JACQUELINE. Well, any luck with Alan? (*She sits on the* L. *edge of the table* C.)

DIANA (*shortly*). No.

JACQUELINE. He wouldn't listen to reason?

DIANA. Do you mind, Jacqueline? I'm really too upset to talk about it.

JACQUELINE. Why don't you go to England with him, if you feel like that.

DIANA. How can I go chasing him across half a continent? One has a little pride, after all.

JACQUELINE. Yes, I suppose one has.

DIANA. Besides, if Alan really feels he'll be happier without me, there's nothing I can do about it.

JACQUELINE. No, I suppose there isn't. (*Inconsequentially.*) Poor Lord Heybrook!

DIANA (*rising and crossing to the window up* R.). What's Lord Heybrook got to do with it?

JACQUELINE. Nothing. It's a lovely morning for a bathe, don't you think? There's a cold wind and the sea is rough, but I shouldn't let that stop you.

DIANA. Really, Jacqueline, you're becoming quite nice and catty. (*Defiantly.*) As a matter of fact, I think I will have a bathe. Why don't you come with me ?

JACQUELINE. Oh, no. My bathing-dress isn't nearly attractive enough. Besides, I'm giving lessons all the morning. (*Looking at her watch.*) I'm supposed to be giving one now. Kit's late as usual.

DIANA (*coming to between chairs* 2 *and* 3). By the way, how are you getting on in that direction ?

JACQUELINE. Not very well, I'm afraid.

DIANA. Oh, I'm sorry. I suppose Kit's terribly upset about me ?

JACQUELINE (*rising and crossing up* R.). You needn't worry. I shall do my best to console him.

DIANA. I've been horribly unkind to him. Oh, well, when Alan's gone I shall have to be specially nice to him to make up for it.

JACQUELINE (*alarmed*). Oh, no.

(DIANA *raises her eyebrows.*)

Oh, why don't you go to England with Alan ? Heaven knows Alan's never done me any harm, but I can feel quite ruthless about anything that will get you out of this house.

DIANA. Excitable race you French—I always say.

(KIT *comes in up* L.)

KIT (*ignoring* DIANA). Sorry, Jack. I'm late.

JACQUELINE. All right, Kit. (*She comes to chair* 2 *and sits.*)

DIANA. Oh, well, don't let me disturb you. (*Going to the door up* L.) I'm going to have a bathe.

(*She goes out.* KIT *stands shyly, holding a notebook.*)

JACQUELINE (*adopting a schoolmistress manner*). Sit down, Kit.

(KIT *sits in chair* 4.)

Have you done that work I set you ?

(*He hands her his notebook.*)

Good. You must have worked quite hard.

(*She bends her head over the notebook.* KIT *gazes at her.*)

KIT (*suddenly*). Jack, I want to say——

JACQUELINE (*hurriedly*). This is wrong. (*She underlines a word.*) You can't say that in French. You have to turn it. (*She writes something in the book.*) Do you see ?

KIT (*looking over her shoulder*). Yes. I see.

(JACQUELINE *continues to read.*)

JACQUELINE. My dear Kit—— (*Reading.*) Une pipe remplie avec du tabac. What ought it to be ?

KIT. Remplie de tabac, of course.

JACQUELINE. Why didn't you write it, then ? (*She underlines another word.*) Kit, this whole exercise is terrible. What on earth were you thinking of when you did it ?

KIT. You.

JACQUELINE. Well, you'd better do it again.

KIT (*annoyed*). What! Do it all again ?

JACQUELINE. Yes. (*Weakening.*) Why were you thinking of me ?

KIT. Not the whole damn thing ?

JACQUELINE. Certainly. Why were you thinking of me ?

KIT (*with dignity*). Shall I translate you some La Bruyère ? (*He hands her a La Bruyère book.*)

JACQUELINE. All right.

KIT. Page one hundred and eight.

(*They take up their books in a dignified silence.*)

JACQUELINE. If I let you off, will you tell me ?

KIT. I might.

JACQUELINE. Very well. You're let off. Only mind you, if you do another exercise as bad as that I'll make you do it again and three more besides. Now, why were you thinking of me ?

KIT. I was wondering whether I ought to tell you I was sorry for—for what happened last night, or whether I ought to pass it off with a gay laugh and a shrug of the shoulders.

JACQUELINE. Which did you decide ?

KIT. I decided to leave it to you.

JACQUELINE. I think I'd rather have the gay laugh and the shrug of the shoulders.

KIT. You shall have it. (*He gets up.*)

JACQUELINE. No, you needn't bother. We'll take the gay laugh, etcetera, for granted.

KIT (*sitting*). Very well. The incident is now closed, permanently and perpetually closed. Chapter Four. Of love. There is a fragrance in pure friendship.

JACQUELINE (*puzzled at his attitude*). I don't know why you should have thought I wanted you to apologize. After all, what's a kiss between friends ?

KIT. Alan told me this morning that you were in a steaming fury with me about it, so I thought——

JACQUELINE. Oh, I see. Alan's been talking to you about me this morning, has he ? Come on, tell me, what's he been saying now ?

KIT. I don't see why I shouldn't tell you. You see, last night, when Alan was a bit drunk, he played a stupid practical joke on me. He told me (*covering his face with his hands*)—this is a bit embarrassing, but it's a good laugh—he told me that you had been madly in love with me for two months. (*He uncovers his face and waits for the laugh which doesn't come.*) Well, I, being also rather drunk, believed him, and so, as I was feeling rather sentimental, I—kissed you, as you remember; and of course I couldn't understand why you didn't fall into my arms and say, " At last, at last ! " or some such rot. However, this morning Alan told me the whole thing had been a joke, and that you were really rather angry with me for—well—spoiling a beautiful friendship and all that nonsense. So that's why I thought I'd better apologize.

JACQUELINE (*with sudden violence*).   What a blasted fool Alan is !

KIT.   Yes, it was a damn silly trick to play.   Not at all like him.

JACQUELINE.   Kit—supposing I—had fallen into your arms and said, " At last, at last ! " or some such rot, what would you have done ?

KIT.   Oh, I should have kissed you again and said : " I've loved you all the time without knowing it," or some such idiocy.

JACQUELINE.   Oh, Kit.   You wouldn't.

KIT (*apologetically*).   Well, I told you I was feeling sentimental last night, and what with seeing what a fool I'd been over Diana and trying to forget her, and suddenly hearing that you were in love with me, and being drunk——

JACQUELINE.   You don't feel sentimental this morning, do you ?

KIT.   Lord, no.   You don't have to worry any more.   I'm quite all right now.   (*He takes up his book and tries to concentrate.*)

JACQUELINE.   Isn't there any chance of your feeling sentimental again, sometime ?

KIT.   Oh, no.   You're quite safe.

JACQUELINE.   If I gave you a drink or two, and told you that what Alan said last night was the truth ?   And that I have been in love with you for two months and that I've been longing for you to kiss me every time I'm with you—would that make you feel sentimental ?

KIT.   There's no knowing what it mightn't make me feel.

(*There is a pause.*)

JACQUELINE.   I haven't got any drink, Kit.   Or must you have drink ?

(KIT *rises to sit in chair* 3 *and embraces her.*)

(*A little hysterically.*)   At last, at last !

KIT.   I've loved you all the time without knowing it.

JACQUELINE.   Or some such idiocy.

KIT.   I mean that, Jack.

JACQUELINE.   Don't get serious, please, Kit.   This is only a joke. It's only because we are both feeling a bit sentimental at the same time.   (*Holding him away.*)   Or are you ?

KIT. Would I be behaving like this if I weren't?

JACQUELINE. I don't know. I wouldn't like to have played a sort of Diana trick on you. You haven't got that trapped feeling, have you?

KIT. I've got a peculiar feeling in the stomach, and an odd buzzing noise in the head. I think that must mean I'm in love with you.

JACQUELINE. You mustn't talk about love.

KIT. But you do.

JACQUELINE. I've got two months' start of you. I'm not going to let you mention the word love for two months. (*She puts her arm round his shoulder.*) Oh, Kit, do you think there's a chance you may be feeling sentimental in two months' time?

KIT. I'll take ten to one.

JACQUELINE. Well, go on being beastly to me in the meanwhile, because I should hate it if you didn't.

KIT. I'll try, but it won't be easy.

(ALAN *pokes his head cautiously round the door up* L.)

JACQUELINE. Come in, Alan. You're quite safe and I've got some news.

(ALAN *comes in, followed by* ROGERS. *They both have a suitcase.* ALAN *is carrying a hat.*)

ALAN. What news?

(ALAN *puts his suitcase and hat up stage* L. ROGERS *puts the other suitcase down* L.)

JACQUELINE. I don't want the Commander to hear it. (*To* ROGERS.) Do you mind awfully?

ROGERS. Oh, no. Not at all. Tell me when you're finished.

(*He goes out up* L.)

ALAN. Well, what's the news?

JACQUELINE. Kit says it's just possible that in two months' time he may feel quite sentimental about me.

(ALAN *comes between them.*)

ALAN. Well, well, well. You could knock me over with a feather.

KIT. You've got a lot to explain, Alan. What the hell do you mean by telling me a whole packet of lies?

ALAN. Is that the proper way to speak to one, who, by a series of tortuous ruses, has at last brought you two love-birds together?

JACQUELINE. We're not love-birds. We're friends.

KIT. Sentimental friends.

JACQUELINE. No. Friends who sometimes feel sentimental.

ALAN. Well, make up your minds what you are. Time presses. I came in to say good-bye.

ROGERS (*appearing in the doorway*). I can come in now, can't I ?
(*He comes down* L.)

JACQUELINE. How did you know ?

ROGERS. Male intuition as distinct from the female brand. I
listened at the keyhole.

ALAN (*going to* ROGERS). Do you know, Jack, the only reason
I'm sorry to be going is having to leave Bill just when I'd discovered
him.

ROGERS. We'll see each other again, don't you worry. We're
brothers under the skin.

ALAN. Tell me, Jack, did Diana say anything about coming to
England with me ?

JACQUELINE. No, she's definitely staying here. She says your
happiness comes first.

ALAN. For my happiness read Lord Heybrook. Thank God for
His Lordship.

(*He moves up* L. KENNETH *enters up* L.)

KENNETH. Alan, must you go ?

ALAN. Yes, Babe, I must. There's a load off my mind, and I
don't only mean Diana.

KENNETH. I don't think you know what you're doing.

ALAN. Oh, yes, I do.

(*The noise of a car is heard outside.* MAINGOT *appears at the window
up* R.)

MAINGOT. Jacqueline, Jacqueline. Je crois que c'est Lord Heybrook qui arrive. Es-tu prête ?

JACQUELINE. Oui, Papa.

MAINGOT. Bien !

(*He exits again.*)

JACQUELINE. Lord Heybrook ! Oh, go and tell Diana, someone,
or she'll miss her entrance.

(BRIAN *comes in up* L. *and goes to the window down* R.)

KIT (*running to the door up* L.). Diana, Lord Heybrook ! (*He
returns and sits on the floor by the armchair down* R.)

JACQUELINE. What does he look like, Kenneth ?

KENNETH. I can't see. Your father is in the light.

ALAN. Oh, sit down, all of you. Give the man a chance ! (*He
sits in chair* 1.)

(KENNETH *goes on to the steps in the window.* ROGERS *sits on the sofa
in the alcove.* JACQUELINE *sits in the armchair down* R.)

MAINGOT (*calling off*). Marianne ! Les bagages !

(DIANA *enters and stands* L. *of the bookcase.*)

Par ici, milord.

(MAINGOT *enters through the window with* LORD HEYBROOK. *The latter is a bright young schoolboy of about fifteen. He carries his straw hat.*)

(*Escorting* LORD HEYBROOK *across to the door up* L.)   Alors vous êtes bien arrivé. J'éspère que vous avez fait bon voyage . . .

(They go out L.)

DIANA.   Come and help me pack, someone. I'm going to catch that London train or die.

(*All but* ALAN *rise and burst out laughing.* DIANA *disappears through the door up* L. ALAN *rises and crosses up* C.)

ALAN (*pursuing her despairingly, then turning at the door*). Stop laughing, you idiots. It isn't funny. It's a bloody tragedy.

(But they only laugh the louder.)

CURTAIN.

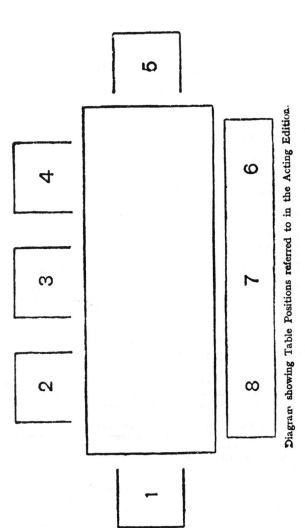

Diagram showing Table Positions referred to in the Acting Edition.

PROPERTY PLOT

(As used at the Criterion Theatre)

ACT I

Green felt over stage.
1 large striped rug below table c.
1 small striped rug in front of French windows up ʀ.
1 small striped rug in front of double doors up ʟ.
At window down ʀ. :
    1 pair pink and white curtains.
    1 pink and white pelmet.
    1 pair pink and white sashes.
1 red and white striped sunblind outside window down ʀ.
At French window up ʀ. :
    1 pair pink and white curtains.
    1 pink and white pelmet.
    1 pair pink and white sashes.
1 red and white striped sunblind outside French window up ʀ.
1 coloured tint in oval frame on wall down ʀ.
2 tints (1 large and 1 small) in black oblong frames under electric bracket ʀ.ᴄ.
2 tints (1 large and 1 small) in black oblong frames under electric bracket ʟ.ᴄ.
1 coloured tint in round frame between two doors ʟ.
1 tint in black frame between two doors ʟ.
1 Curot oil painting in oblong gilt frame over door down ʟ.
1 oval miniature in gilt frame below door down ʟ.
1 plaster plaque (Nun) below door down ʟ.
1 workable French telephone on wall between doors ʟ.
Bookcase up ᴄ. with rows of books—all French.
    On top shelf : 1 plaster bust, 1 pink and white china vase, 1 globe of world.
    On bottom shelf : half-row of books, 1 china plate, 2 blue china vases, 1
        brass inkstand ; 1 workbasket with needles, 2 reels of green silk, tape-
        measure and various sewing requirements.
1 plum-coloured upholstered mahogany stool down ʀ.
1 walnut kidney-shaped table in window down ʀ. with 3 French magazines
    and 1 exercise-book.
1 wooden lamp standard with shade between windows ʀ.
1 soft armchair and red and white striped cover, with 1 plum-coloured cushion,
    down ʀ.ᴄ.
1 footstool covered same as curtains below armchair down ʀ.ᴄ.
1 round mahogany table and under shelf up ʀ., with 1 large vase, 1 bunch
    of assorted flowers, 1 fruit-dish filled with apples and bananas, 1 filled
    wooden cigarette-box, 1 matchstand, 1 matchbox in case, 1 ashtray. 3
    magazines on under shelf.
1 antique sofa with 2 cushions of same material as curtains in bookcase alcove.
1 walnut table between doors ʟ. with 1 glass vase, 1 bunch of sweet peas,
    1 enamel ashtray, with various cutlery in top drawer.
1 antique armchair to match sofa, with red and white striped cushion, down ʟ.
1 long oak table in ᴄ. of set with 1 yellow and white check tablecloth, 6 clean
    yellow cups and saucers, 6 teaspoons, 1 used cup and saucer, 1 teaspoon,
    5 clean small plates, 5 clean small knives, 2 used small knives, 1 butter

dish with butter and butter knife, 6 ivory table-napkin rings, 2 silver
table-napkin rings, 8 white and yellow check table-napkins, 1 glass ashtray, 1 brown china coffee-pot (filled), 1 brown china milk-jug (filled),
1 breadbasket with 8 rolls of horse-shoe-shape bread, 1 glass toothpick
stand (filled), 1 jam-jar filled with marmalade, 1 jam-spoon, 1 French-
English dictionary, 1 exercise book, 1 pencil, 1 letter for BRIAN, 1 copy
of " Le Matin " for MAINGOT, 1 letter for MAINGOT.
1 red and white striped mahogany chair at L. end of table.
1 red and white striped mahogany chair at R. end of table.
3 red and white striped mahogany chairs above table.
1 plum-coloured upholstered mahogany bench below table.

Off Stage L.
Copy of " The Times " for ALAN.
Tray containing doyley, dish of scrambled eggs, knife and fork, for MARIANNE.
Used cup and saucer for MAINGOT.
Phrase-book, dictionary and exercise-book for ALAN.
2 books of La Bruyère for KIT.

Off Stage R.
2 bath towels for KIT.

Personal.
Watch for MAINGOT.
Filled cigarette-case for ROGERS.
Filled matchbox for ROGERS.
Fountain-pen for ALAN.
Sun-glasses for DIANA.

ACT II

SCENE 1

General setting as Act I.
On table C.: 1 red and white check tablecloth, 8 small blue plates, 8 blue
dessert-plates, 7 dessertspoons (at each place except No. 4), 8 small knives,
1 toothpick-stand (filled), 1 glass dish of prunes, 1 glass ashtray, 1 bottle
of mineral water in silver coaster, 1 bottle of French wine in silver coaster,
1 silver sugar-sifter, 6 ivory table-napkin rings, 2 silver table-napkin rings,
8 red and white check table-napkins, 1 glass tankard (at place No. 4), 7
glass tumblers.
On table down R.: 3 French magazines, KIT's exercise-book, 1 pedestal vase
of roses.
On table L.: remove vase of flowers, check dessertspoon for ROGERS in top
drawer.
On table up R.C.: remove fruit-bowl, change vase and flowers, set workbasket
from bookcase on under shelf.

Off Stage L.
1 large tray each for JACQUELINE and MARIANNE.
2 clean ashtrays for JACQUELINE.
Exercise-book, phrase-book and pencil for ALAN.
Exercise-book, phrase-book and pencil for KENNETH.

Off Stage R.
Parcel containing script and letter inside for BRIAN.
Exercise-book for MAINGOT.

Personal.
Filled cigarette-case for ALAN.
Filled matchbox for ALAN.

SCENE 2

General setting as Act I, with the following alterations :
Set sofa L.C., facing down C.
Remove table C. into alcove and place vase of flowers from table up R. on C. of table. Place 2 ashtrays on table.
Remove table up R. to L. of armchair down R.C. Magazines on table with other props. as previous Act, also check workbasket on under shelf.
Remove table-bench to in front of table up C.
1 small chair R. of bookcase.
2 small chairs L. of bookcase.
2 small chairs struck off set.
Under R. end of table-bench set slippers to fit MAINGOT.

Off Stage L.
ALAN's German coat.
KIT's Grecian coat, to fit ROGERS.

ACT III
SCENE 1

General setting as previous scene.
Set 1 cushion from sofa R. of sofa.
Set 1 ashtray with cigarette-end in on floor at L. end of sofa.
On table L. : 1 bowl of fruit.
On table L. of armchair R.C. : 1 exercise-book and pencil.
Check MAINGOT's slippers under bench up C.

Personal.
43 francs for BRIAN.
Visiting-card for BRIAN.
Cigarette-case (no elastic) with loose cigarettes for KIT.

SCENE 2

General setting as Act I. *N.B.*—Table C. and sofa in alcove.
On table C. : White and yellow check tablecloth ready for folding, 1 tray full of dirty yellow breakfast china for MARIANNE to take off.
Strike small table and contents from L. of armchair down R.C.

Off Stage L.
Suitcase each for ALAN and KENNETH.
Essay sheet with 1 line written and exercise-book for BRIAN
2 La Bruyère books for KIT.

Off Stage R.
Phrase-book and exercise-book for KENNETH.